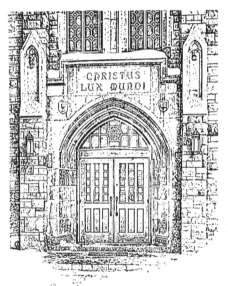

Luther Theological Seminary
ST. PAUL, MINNESOTA

CHRISTUS
LUX MUNDI

EX LIBRIS

THE RATIONAL SOCIETY

THE
RATIONAL
SOCIETY

*A Critical Study of
Santayana's Social Thought*

BETH J. SINGER

1970
The Press of Case Western Reserve University
Cleveland/London

For my family

Foreword

THE POWERFUL LANGUAGE of Santayana, his resourcefulness as a formulator and as a polemicist, make it hard for us to realize that he is an elusive philosopher. And by this I do not mean only that the texture of his reasoning is intricate or that the level of his insight resists immediate grasp. It seems evident enough that the firmness in his mode of statement, the categorical manner and the fluency, aspire to anything but plainness or simplicity. If he is able to respect simplicity as a means (he does profess an underlying allegiance to "common sense"), he can scarcely regard it as commensurate with the demands of philosophic reflection. But the elusiveness, the problem of access to which I am referring, arises from a different and somewhat paradoxical circumstance, namely, that no single work of Santayana's conveys the full import of his perspective despite the fact that each seems to do precisely this and even to embody all of his central themes. The appeal of the individual works, their expository finish, deceives us with respect to the character of the philosophic structure as a whole. The entanglements and the fluctuations which enter into this structure are most readily discerned from the relation of the works to one another and from their intended role as components of a grand product. Eventually we are able to discern the less than perfect harmony within the components themselves. We need, then, to be alert to what the systematic Santayana is presupposing in each of his works, and we need to study in each the reciprocal influence between the system and its application at hand, as Professor Singer has done in the area she has chosen to investigate.

Santayana, if I may so put it, is more than systematic—or systematic not only in the sense of shaping categories with wide scope and applying them recurrently to a variety of issues but in another and quite ingenuous sense. To him nothing, however common or commonplace, falls outside the pale of philosophic interpretation. There is no subject in which he cannot find and enunciate generalized significance, a significance continuous with that of his conceptual framework as the latter is developed abstractly. And this is a kind of scope which surprisingly few systems achieve, no matter how many may claim it. For it is not primarily in the fertility of concepts as such that this kind of scope lies: many systems, in a purely technical sense, can boast an applicability of their categories to whatever there is, and Santayana's own formal categories are not among the most stimulating or exciting. The fertility is that of the philosopher who can breathe life and pulsation into systemic elements. Santayana might have preferred to say merely that in anything which is of human concern we can discover some possible bearing on the good and the beautiful. Those who distrust his method of observing, of analyzing, or of building often tend to think of him as proliferating metaphors. Suffice it to note that if such an opinion ever was entertained by his peers, men like Russell and Moore as well as Whitehead and Dewey, it did not diminish their regard for him or affect his impact upon them.

Professor Singer's way of recognizing Santayana in his quest of generic significance for the great and the small alike is to depict him as metaphysician of human experience and culture. She exhibits the connection between the assumptions of his general ontology and what she calls his metaphysics of society, so that the former is seen as a condition of the latter's intelligibility. At the same time, through translation into social and political terms, the tissue of the ontology is revealed by her in an unexpected light, its strengths and weaknesses made vivid. Understanding the importance of Santayana (partly as representing a breadth of outlook crucial for the future of philosophy) and able to distinguish his objectives, she eschews criticisms which are trivial or predatory, devoting a major portion of her critical endeavor to tracing intentions and examining consequences. Whether or not it is true that Santayana relies more heavily upon metaphors than do philosophers of comparable stature—Professor Singer is not troubled by this question, and neither am I—it is reassuringly true that she takes metaphors no less seriously than any other philosophic strategy for the discrimination of traits in the world. This discipline of detachment necessarily results in the clarification not only of views which are distinctively Santayana's but of subjects common to Santayana and others, such as the philosophic commitments latent in political conservatism.

In her integration of the ideas and attitudes that define Santayana's metaphysics of politics, Professor Singer has focussed most sharply on the two major relevant works, *Reason in Society* and *Dominations and Powers,* published almost half a century apart. Though aware of the problems which such a span of time ordinarily raises for interpretation, she illuminates each of the two works by weaving them equally into her inquiry. The fresh eye she has cast on them, and in particular her sense of the earlier one's abiding value, somehow revives for me the experience of a course I took many years ago with Morris R. Cohen in the Philosophy of Civilization. The text he used was *Reason in Society.* Once more it has become clear, through the medium of a penetrating study, how profitable it is philosophically to explore the immense insights and the immense difficulties in Santayana's thought.

Justus Buchler

Acknowledgments

I AM GLAD of the opportunity to thank some of the people whose support, guidance, and criticism have helped me so much. I owe my initial interest in Santayana to Joseph L. Blau. Professors Blau, John Herman Randall, Jr., David Sidorsky, and Robert McShea criticized the manuscript. Douglas Greenlee exposed some knotty problems of interpretation. Members of The Philosophical Group of New York read and discussed Chapter VII and were helpful in pointing out sections needing clarification or restatement.

Justus Buchler has scrutinized the text with care. I mean to express more than the mandatory ritual utterance when I claim sole responsibility for its errors or defects. Professor Buchler's preciseness, his sensitive awareness of diverse modes and styles of judgment, and his critical acumen set a standard to which I aspire. I hope the respect for the integrity of philosophy which I learned as his student is visible in my work.

Lester Singer willingly helped me at every stage in the preparation and writing of this book. His contributions, both as a scholar and as my husband, are deeply appreciated. I would like to thank Judi Alper for her help in proofreading. I am also grateful to Eleanor Blau and Barbara Watson for their encouragement.

B. J. S.

Abbreviations

DL	Dialogues in Limbo
DP	Dominations and Powers
EGP	Egotism in German Philosophy
GTB	The Genteel Tradition at Bay
Letters	The Letters of George Santayana
OS	Obiter Scripta
Philosophy	The Philosophy of George Santayana
PSL	Platonism and the Spiritual Life
RA	Reason in Art
RCS	Reason in Common Sense
RM	The Realm of Matter
RR	Reason in Religion
RS	The Realm of Spirit
RSci	Reason in Science
RSoc	Reason in Society
SAF	Scepticism and Animal Faith
SE	Soliloquies in England and Later Soliloquies
STT	Some Turns of Thought in Modern Philosophy

Contents

1. The Natural Philosophy of a Moralist   1
2. Metaphysics of Society   9
3. The Ambiguities of Santayana's Materialism   17
4. Natural Society   32
5. Biology and Civilization   46
6. Moral Idealism and Moral Rationality   59
7. Militancy and the Moral Life   78
8. The Moral Economy   101
9. Santayana's Political Naturalism   121

Index   139

CHAPTER 1

The Natural Philosophy
of a Moralist

IF GEORGE SANTAYANA is not a political theorist in twentieth-century terms, there is nevertheless in his philosophy a distinctive conception of the nature of society and politics, as well as a perspective for political judgment. Some of his more widely publicized political dicta bespeak a narrowness of vision that belies the comprehensiveness and power of this perspective. It is not my purpose to defend Santayana, but to analyze critically the foundations of his philosophy of society and politics. In the course of this analysis it should become clear that, whether or not one accepts his doctrines or the premises on which they rest, Santayana is to be regarded as a systematic social philosopher. I hope it will also become evident that despite weaknesses in both the metaphysical substructure and the more specifically political dimensions of his philosophy, Santayana enunciates a system of highly general and useful categories by means of which he tries to account for and do justice to the manifold forms which society and culture take on. That these categories are philosophic rather than scientific is not, I believe, a function of the categories themselves, but of the context in which they acquire significance. Santayana's ethical and political categories may have scientific import, as has been acknowledged by J. J. Faurot in an interesting and sympathetic paper in a journal of political science.[1] Even political science, for Santayana, would be symbolic rather than literally true, for this is a limitation he attributes to all knowledge. But, like Plato and Aristotle, he views political philosophy and ethics as practical rather than purely theoretical disciplines. Taken this way, as developing and interpreting *ideals*, politics is closer to religion and to poetry than to science. The real irony of Santayana's politics, however, is that in the end he does not rationally justify commitment to any ideal, nor does his metaphysics allow political ideals, or those of religion or poetry, to be efficacious in the lives of the men who conceive them.

While a comprehensive exposition of Santayana's philosophic system is not within the compass of this book, I will try to exhibit the systematic rela-

1

tions of his social philosophy in order to make it intelligible and accessible to significant criticism. Santayana himself indicated that this is how his social philosophy is to be read. Many of what he considered to be the misconstructions of his late, comprehensive work, *Dominations and Powers,* he attributed to ignorance of the philosophy in which he asserted it to be embedded.[2,3] In trying to do justice to it, then, and to his social philosophy as a whole, one should, in his own words, begin with its vital foundation in his philosophy and proceed to its corollaries.[4] Santayana seems to have believed his philosophy to have been almost universally misunderstood, and he took pains to reply to his "friendly critics," for instance in his *Soliloquies in England* and his own essays in the volume of *The Library of Living Philosophers* devoted to his work.[5,6]

In fact, I find it impossible to understand Santayana's social philosophy except as an integral part of his natural and moral philosophy. He conceives society as being part of nature and governed by the same principles. In general, Santayana identifies nature with physical existence. In his system, strictly speaking, nothing supernatural or non-natural exists. By "nature" Santayana most often means the system of processes which he assumes gives rise to all consciousness and all values, all ends, aims, and ideals, and which he identifies with the realm of matter. The "being" of essences is not "existence"; and while spirit is not physical, it is defined here as the awakening of an organism to consciousness, not as a substance. Spirit and mind, for Santayana, do belong to "nature" in an extended sense. If, as Santayana believes, essences come to be embodied in matter; and if, as he also believes, essences are "given" as data of intuition; then essences, too, would seem to belong to nature. Their status in Santayana's metaphysics is ambiguous. In certain contexts, notably in his critique of Kant in *Reason in Common Sense,* Santayana defines "nature" as the totality of objects of possible experience. Some of the difficulties entailed by this doctrine, and certain other problems in Santayana's concept of nature, will be exposed in the chapters to come.

Like Aristotle, Santayana distinguishes between "nature" and "art," but also like Aristotle, he takes art to be continuous with nature. Man, who by art tries to improve upon nature, is never set over against the natural world. Reason is considered a harmony of natural powers rather than a supernatural gift. Physical nature, according to Santayana, generates life, awareness, and society. For beings who are aware of their aims and of the impact of some existents upon others, nature takes on a moral dimension. Societies in particular have ramifications which Santayana calls moral: benevolent or malign consequences in the lives of their members or in the lives of other societies. Regardless of the turns his thinking takes from time to time, Santayana never ceases to see society as continuous with its more inclusive natural context and never ceases to be concerned about the effects of political and cultural developments in the lives of men.

Santayana is a "conservative." The word is applied to his political philosophy because of the value he places on tradition, his suspicion of programmatic reform, and his attacks upon "liberalism." But there is no evidence that his conservatism is primarily, if at all, an inheritance from conservative political thinkers like Burke, nor does he consistently adhere to the views conventionally classed as "conservative." What I prefer to call Santayana's political naturalism, like his moral naturalism in general, grows out of his ontological speculations. For this reason, and because of his expressed wish, part of what follows deals directly with the "metaphysical foundations" of Santayana's social thought, that is, with his "naturalism," or "materialism" as he frequently calls it, which will be critically analyzed, both from the point of view of its content and that of its justification.

Despite his opposition to moralizing in speculative philosophy, and in fact consistently with it, Santayana is a moral philosopher in the deepest sense of the term. Whereas he denies that the universe is intrinsically moral and that it is governed by purposes or ethical principles, he conceives it to be a moral cosmos as well as a physical one, a world *within* which interests are generated, where they harmonize or conflict, and where reflection in the service of interest lends value and distinction to what would otherwise be brute existence. And it is the moral drama rather than the physical process which is his main concern. In Santayana's consideration of this moral cosmos, two perspectives intersect, one speculative and systematic, the other critical. In the first place, he tries to analyze and to account for human experience per se: this is the perspective which dominates his ontology, or speculative physics, and its articulation in terms of the realms of being. In addition, ontology subserves another end: in Santayana's philosophy of civilization (and his entire philosophy may be seen as culminating in a philosophy of civilization), he scrutinizes human institutions, evaluating them in the light of their products and their potentialities, studying and criticizing the "ideals" they generate and the movements to which these ideals are central.

Just as Santayana sees in the Platonic Ideas a vision of the aspiration of existence to perfection and considers Plato's doctrine to be a moral, not a metaphysical one, I see his own "Platonist" focus on "ideal realizations" as constituting a moral interest in the natural world.[7] He claims that his point of view is that of common sense, and that "common sense is not more convinced of anything than of the difference between good and evil, advantage and disaster; and it cannot dispense with a moral interpretation of the universe."[8] In his doctine of essences, Santayana strips Plato's Ideas of power; but they retain their attractiveness and their worth. For him the forms of things are more important than the things themselves; they are "ideal" in the dual sense of "intelligible" and "admirable." The universe is not created or governed by the Good, on his view, but the idea that the Good is determined by it renders the world morally significant.

In *The Life of Reason,* Santayana draws the outlines of a natural history of human institutions and arts, indicating, on the one hand, the biologic and economic origins of civilization, and, on the other, assessing the major cultural achievements in the light of his understanding of nature and human nature.[9] His dual interest (both metaphysical and moral) in society and its institutions is exemplified and discussed in the analysis of social science in *Reason in Science.* There it is said, for example, that political economy may be either descriptive or "dialectical." That is to say, its subject matter can be treated factually or morally; when it is treated morally, it is in the effort to judge what course of conduct would be right. In this case, where the political economist is determining a policy (and here is the root meaning of "politics"), he is not dedicated to the study of actual movements and tendencies so much as to searching out and formulating his own intent.[10] Santayana is always both a naturalist and a moralist, a theoretician and a judge, and strives to be both simultaneously so that each role will enrich the other.

Dominations and Powers, more heavily concerned with politics than with culture, exhibits the same double approach, which Santayana characteristically acknowledges:

> . . . I am guided by an analytic and moral interest, not by any merely descriptive or anthropological theory. . . . and the interest that guides the moral philosopher is less to trace the passage of mankind from one type of organisation to another, than to distinguish in each type the good and the evil that it comports: in other words to disentangle the Powers at work in that civilisation and mark the Domination that one or another of them may exercise over the rest.[11]

The distinction between "dominations" and "powers" is itself a moral one.[12] In this book society is pictured as a field of striving and conflicting organisms, at once dependent upon and competing with one another for the means of survival and growth. Every element in that moral universe is a power, but any power becomes a domination from the viewpoint of another power which it thwarts. In this setting, domination is inevitable since the physical world continually generates new growths without regard for the interests of those already in existence. The pluralism exhibited in this doctrine leads Santayana to an acceptance of diversity itself as the only legitimate political aim. Life itself, though he views it as natural and hence bound by the laws of nature at large, diverges from many centers. Therefore, any ideal, since it emanates from and expresses a single tendency in a crowded world, is doomed to at least partial failure. "Thus the formal perfection of the universe, as completely expressing its own nature and laws, covers a moral chaos, in which the vital nature or law of each thing is defeated and turned into a maimed and monstrous caricature of what that thing was capable of becoming."[13]

The normative and descriptive dimensions of Santayana's philosophy are interdependent and rest on the same assumptions: at every point his criticism is rooted in his materialism; his moral philosophy is naturalistic; and his natural philosophy is focussed on the ideal phenomena in which, despite his growing pessimism, he continues in all his writings to find the meaning and worth of existence. While he pursues both, Santayana follows Hume in distinguishing sharply between scientific and critical analysis of the moral life. What he would call the "natural science" of morality is descriptive and explanatory of actual evaluations. His writings about society and civilization fall, in part, into this class. Santayana believes that the explanation of actual occurrences, including valuations, must ultimately be biological or physical: "Why anyone values anything at all, or anything in particular, is a question of physics."[14] The natural science of morality, and social science with it, is a branch of physics. In contrast, "ethics" (sometimes ambiguously called "moral science") is properly part of "natural morality," an embodiment of volition, not a description of it.[15] That is, ethics tries to decide what is right; moral science, properly so called, to discover what is thought to be right and why. "Rational ethics" is a development of natural morality, which is defined in *Reason in Science* as a systematic articulation of natural impulses, the "real needs" of a creature. This process is akin to the Socratic method, a dialectic of the Will.[16] Defining "good" in terms of the relation between existing need and fulfillment, Santayana says, "What ethics asks is not why a thing is good, but whether it is good or not."[17] *The Life of Reason,* then, in its critical aspect, is conceived as part of his own rational ethics. In "sketching the ground-plan of a true commonwealth," that is, in stating what he thinks are truly adequate and just foundations of a humane and universally satisfying culture, Santayana believes himself to be continuing the tradition of Socrates, Plato, and Aristotle.[18] To the extent that it, too, is diagnostic and prescriptive, *Dominations and Powers* is also an ethical treatise; like Plato and Aristotle again, Santayana conceives ethics and politics to constitute a single discipline.

As Santayana interprets Hume, the proposition that morality is not founded on reason entails that it is founded on instinct, i.e., the persistent impulses of living creatures. This assumption is the basis of his moral naturalism. What is, on this view, is not merely one source of what ought to be: there could be no other, so that rational ethics consists in the application of "the logic of practice" to information provided by experience and corrected by science concerning actual needs and tendencies. This Socratic dialectic leads to the definition of ideals, the determination of what ought to be and to be done. "Moral rationality" as defined in *Reason in Science* consists in so judging and in acting in accordance with ends so adjudicated rather than on the basis of spontaneous moral perception. But the justification of ends, however rational, and hence the justification of ethics, remains their foundation in impulse. Thus the final court of appeals for normative philosophy is science, which studies and explains impulse.

The highest form of moral rationality for Santayana in *The Life of Reason* is "moral idealism," the direction of life toward an inclusive ideal. To conceive the whole of life to be oriented toward an ideal is "spirituality," in one of his early senses of the term: "A man is spiritual when he lives in the presence of the ideal, and whether he eat or drink does so for the sake of a true and ultimate good."[19] When men discovered that moral idealism failed to provide a workable adjustment to this world, disillusioned, "post-rational" moralities or religions arose, which taught that if there is any true and ultimate good for man it must lie outside the realm of the existent. Stoicism and Christianity console the spirit without raising its hopes for happiness in this life.[20] Santayana's own critical philosophy takes on, in his later works, more of a Stoic orientation; yet it should become apparent in the sequel that, as he claims, he never became less of a naturalist in morals. As he grew older, even though he retained many prejudices, Santayana seems to have gained increasing distance from parochial concerns and provincial interests, and to have concluded that, since men and societies vary, different types of social order may be equally valid or nearly so. The viewpoint of *Dominations and Powers* may be characterized as "disillusioned" in that it no longer illustrates the effort to discover a single, universally acceptable ideal of civilization or of political or economic rationality. Instead Santayana prescribes an ideal to which diversity itself is central. His disillusion also takes the form of open acceptance of the inevitability of conflict and defeat. Santayana's position in *Dominations and Powers* is linked to a changed idea of rationality, not to a "post-rational" or "mystical" substitution of sheer aestheticism for reason. It is the concepts of perfect harmony and universality which have been abandoned, not the attempt at moral rationality. And the principle of Santayana's moral philosophy remains the naturalist one that all good and all right are rooted in the essential constitution and aspirations of living beings. Santayana always considered spirituality to be a good, and in later life found in it the only untarnished benefit; but even the detached contemplation of essences (to which the term "spirituality" most frequently refers in Santayana's late works) is the act of an animal and a good *for him*.

In its evolution, Santayana's political naturalism culminates in the thesis that men ought to choose their own ends and formulate their own ideals, even though they will never outgrow the need to be governed. The way of life that is good for one will not be so for another unless the two are closely similar; and that is the case, he claims, only where they share in both natural endowment and history. Increasingly, as he grew older, Santayana conceived the proper viewpoint of the moral philosopher to resemble that of the scientist in its detachment: the philosopher ought to try to understand and appreciate all characters and all ideals, rather than legislate for other men goals which reflect his own character and his own circumstances. But Santayana never advocated abandonment of the normative dimension of philosophy. It will be part of my task to trace some of the connections between Santayana's generalizations about nature and his criticisms of movements and doctrines, to assess the adequacy of the former and consider the virtues of the latter.

NOTES

[1] "The Political Thought of George Santayana," *Western Political Quarterly*, XIV (Spring, 1961), 663–75.

[2] *Dominations and Powers* (New York: Charles Scribner's Sons, 1951). Hereafter cited as *DP*.

[3] Cf. letter to Mrs. David Little, November 25, 1951, reproduced in Daniel Cory, ed., *The Letters of George Santayana* (New York: Charles Scribner's Sons, 1955), pp. 423–24. Hereafter cited as *Letters*.

[4] Cf. "Apologia Pro Mente Sua," in Paul Arthur Schilpp, ed., *The Philosophy of George Santayana* (Evanston: Northwestern University Press, 1940), p. 503. Hereafter cited as *Philosophy*.

[5] *Soliloquies in England and Later Soliloquies* (New York: Charles Scribner's Sons, 1922), pp. 245–59. Hereafter cited as *SE*.

[6] "Apologia Pro Mente Sua," in *Philosophy*, p. 503.

[7] "The ideas, which were essentially moral functions, were many and eternal. . . ." *Reason in Religion* (New York: Charles Scribner's Sons, 1905), p. 132. Hereafter cited as *RR*.

[8] *Some Turns of Thought in Modern Philosophy: Five Essays* (London: Cambridge University Press, 1933), p. 14. Hereafter cited as *STT*.

[9] *"The Life of Reason or The Phases of Human Progress"* is the title of the complete work comprising *Reason in Common Sense, Reason in Society, Reason in Religion, Reason in Art,* and *Reason in Science* (New York: Charles Scribner's Sons, 1905–6). Since in this work Santayana refers to Oriental civilizations infrequently and with little detailed analysis

(although one may see their influence in some of his doctrines), it might be more accurate to say he is only concerned with Western civilization, but, like Hegel (he even considered himself to be correcting Hegel), he is trying to write a critical metaphysics or phenomenology of culture and to generalize his categories and judgments to cover all civilizations.

[10] *Reason in Science* (New York: Charles Scribner's Sons, 1906), pp. 99–100. Hereafter cited as *RSci*.

[11] *DP*, p. 26.

[12] Santayana is not consistent in his use of initial capital letters for the names of important categories. For the sake of simplicity, they will be written in lowercase here, except where a term is used in two senses and one is distinguished by a capital as, for example, "Will" and "will." For the same reason, after their introduction, the terms he uses to designate important concepts or categories will usually be used without quotation marks.

[13] *DP*, p. 181.

[14] *RSci*, p. 214.

[15] *Ibid.*, p. 244.

[16] *Ibid.*, p. 213.

[17] *Ibid.*, p. 215.

[18] *Ibid.*, pp. 239–50.

[19] *RR*, p. 193.

[20] Cf. *RSci*, Chapter X, "Post-Rational Morality."

CHAPTER 2

Metaphysics of Society

THOUGH THEY LARGELY OVERLAP, *The Life of Reason* is primarily a philosophy of civilization, whereas *Dominations and Powers* is primarily a philosophy of politics. By "politics," Santayana means "what relates to policy and to polity—to the purposes of human cooperation and the constitution of society," rather than the "meaner" concern with "the *instruments* of policy only, as for instance . . . the form of government or . . . the persons who shall carry it on."[1] The latter may be called politics in the narrow or strict sense. Santayana is a political philosopher in the broad sense of one who is concerned with exposing the sources of the main currents of civilization and with evaluating the ways in which the dominant modes of social organization, religion, art, and inquiry affect the outlook and the progress of the peoples among whom they evolved. In general, the concern with the constitution of society and the evolution of culture, as in *The Life of Reason,* will here be labeled "social philosophy," and questions of policy will be referred to as "political." On occasion, the term "social philosophy" will also refer inclusively to both, as will the term "politics," in accord with Santayana's own usage.

In both political and social philosophy, as in metaphysics, Santayana proclaimed himself a "naturalist," implying both that he considered himself a natural philosopher, in the ancient sense, and that he was a materialist rather than an idealist. Politics, like every other subject, can be studied from the point of view of a naturalist or that of a moralist. Even the formal disciplines may be considered, in the light of their applicability and their normative function, a moral concern. In *Dominations and Powers* Santayana explains that he wants to present both a "materialist interpretation of politics" and "a moral judgment upon it."[2] The hypothesis of materialism governs the latter task as well, and I propose to show that this conjunction leads to a distinctive political philosophy. In developing the consequences of natural philosophy for moral judgment and in attempting to define a consistently naturalistic ethical position, *Dominations and Powers* is continuous with *The Life of Reason.* But in the lesson it draws from naturalism the latter work represents a markedly different political stance.

9

Both of these books approach the natural philosophy of society genetically, and in both the natural history of society is portrayed in terms of the need of the individual for care and for self-realization. Neither work pretends to be literal, yet both are intended to exhibit the motive power which generates a social system, and so they are to be considered scientific. Natural philosophy as Santayana practiced it is both descriptive and speculative. Like psychology and history, it is partly literary, describing as it does pertinent aspects of human experience. "Science—I am speaking of natural science, not of mathematics or philology—is the study of *nature;* the description of *experience* is literature."[3] In common with history and psychology, social science and social philosophy involve the imaginative representation and comparison of types and portions of experience. To be studied and compared, experience must be portrayed imaginatively because it cannot be actually reproduced. Even if it could be shared or repeated, there would be no way of comparing two instances of "the same" experience, since for Santayana each is "essentially invisible, immeasurable, fugitive, and private."[4] Thus, to the extent that the scientist or philosopher generalizes concerning experience, to the extent that he tries to describe social experience or common human experience, he is setting forth a product of his own imagination, just as he would were he to write a novel. The case is the same for psychology, history, the social sciences, and philosophy. The only test of their validity is in the experience of other persons, which they alone can observe and report.

This is not to deny the possibility of behavioral science. If we may use Santayana's analysis of history as a model, each of these disciplines incorporates factual reporting, "story-telling," and "theorizing." The establishment of facts, through remembered and corroborated experience, is the start of natural science. Social and psychological science deal, not with the course of experience itself, but with that which has been experienced, with what has happened and, in some cases, is likely to happen again. A fact is an occurrence *arrested* and *characterized;* it belongs to what Santayana came to call "the realm of truth." Physics, which includes the factual basis of all science, is said to be "the science of existence."[5] But Santayana also holds that "the material element alone is existent, while the ideal element is the sum of all those propositions which are true of what exists materially."[6] Even in being factual, then, physics as he describes it is not in strictness a science of the existent, but of the ideal. The problem of ambiguity in referring to existence, and the confusion between existence and fact, permeate Santayana's metaphysics (as will be shown in Chapter III) despite the fact that he recognizes this and makes terminological reforms. Recognizing the equivocal connotations of his use of the term "existence," he proposes, in *Scepticism and Animal Faith,* to use it "to designate not data of intuition [essences], but facts or events believed to occur in nature."[7] It should become evident in what follows that his use of the term "nature" is as ambiguous as his use of "data," "fact," and "existence."

Science, says Santayana, also has to do with the *conditions* of experience, its background and its source, i.e., with *nature*. Social science, like all science, is a systematic *extension* of experience and common knowledge. History is memory, recorded and *assisted*.[8] Over and above mere reporting, natural history involves the portrayal of typical experiences and the sympathetic reconstruction of past events. This "artificial" extension is based upon hypotheses as to causal connections and underlying forces. Thus, "theorizing" may be said to take place on two levels: (1) that of events and their sequential relations, and (2) that of causation. For Santayana, the guiding hypothesis in all scientific speculation could be none other than that of materialism; in fact, in his "Apologia" he *identifies* physics, scientific speculation, and materialism.[9] Starting with the discriminable properties of experience, Santayana believes we can specify hypothetically those characters and relations of events which a more perfect science would know directly. He is inconsistent on this score, however, claiming, on the one hand, that history is essentially perspectival and theory essential to complete it, and, on the other, that theory "is an expedient to cover ignorance and remedy confusion." A complete history would make theory unnecessary: "The ideal historian, since he would know all the facts, would need no hypotheses, and since he would imagine and hold all events together in their actual juxtapositions he would need no classifications."[10]

The completion of science is also called "metaphysics," even though Santayana repudiates "metaphysics" in certain other senses. "Science may be accepted bodily, while its present results are modified by suggesting speculatively what its ultimate results might be. This is natural philosophy or legitimate metaphysics."[11] In this sense, we are entitled to speak of Santayana's *"metaphysics of society."* As metaphysician he describes observable behavior and organization of men in societies—we might call this social physics and he himself classes it as biology or natural science, acknowledging the role of imagination therein. He tries in addition to reconstruct social experience in the fullness of its moral and historical actuality, an undertaking he classes as literature. Both these endeavors are scientific to the extent that they are verified by other persons who have shared the same experience, though strictly speaking, social science seems to be an ideal which may be only imperfectly approached. "Only when memory is expressed and, in the common field of expression, finds itself corroborated by another memory, does it rise somewhat in dignity and approach scientific knowledge. Two presumptions, when they coincide, make a double assurance."[12] Beyond this, Santayana hypothesizes as to the nature of the existential process of which social and political life are visible and criticizable forms. It is this undertaking that he takes to be eminently philosophical. His preoccupation with both the science and metaphysics of society was lifelong. He considered both concerns to be integral to an interest in nature and to be properly governed by a materialist orientation. In *Dominations and Powers* he sums up the social philosopher's task as that of considering "real events and real forces," which he asserts are "all physical, even when they have a mental and moral accompaniment." Yet the descriptions of these events and forces, the facts which the philosopher of politics deals with, are literary artifacts: "He is composing a drama as it might have been lived." To the extent that he is philosophic, the philosopher will also be concerned with the causes and conditions which are responsible for these facts. That these causes, too, are physical, is said to be "an assumption, or rather a tautology in a naturalistic philosophy."[13]

The assertions that real events, real forces, and causes are all physical are metaphysical assertions in the sense in which Santayana allows the term "metaphysics" to be used. They constitute the foundation of his social and political philosophy in all its stages. As a materialist, Santayana asserts in all his writings the "primacy of nature over spirit in social life."[14] Nature here is to be understood as "physical nature." In both major works on the subject society appears on the scene as part of the physical world. Man is said to be a part of nature, and the organization of nature is taken to be the foundation of his own organization and that of society: "I say that human beings have sprung from the earth. . . . Every sort of creature, every sort of government, will spring up out of the earth, if circumstances only allow it."[15] Whatever arises within the universe is natural, in that it exhibits the potentialities present in the primal order. And that order, for Santayana, is the order of the physical world. Behavior we call political is a complication in the life of organisms, "a purely vegetative growth in the psyche that easily spreads by contagion to a group of psyches and forms a political party or philosophic sect."[16] The evolution and life of society, including all varieties of social change, are assumed by a materialist to rest ultimately upon the interaction of forces, not upon the ideologies of men and movements. At bottom the social order, like the physical order, is a concourse of "atoms fatally combined."[17]

That society has a given form, that social institutions have a particular character, is not taken by Santayana to be consequent upon divine or human purpose or contractual agreement, but rather to be determined by mechanical processes set in motion by chance, that is, by causes not conforming to human reason. Like day and night, society arose out of chaos; but by chaos

Santayana understands "a nature containing none of the objects we are wont to distinguish, a nature such that human life and thought would be impossible in its bosom; but this nature must be presumed to have an order, an order directly importing, if the tendency of its movement be taken into account, all the complexities and beauties, all the sense and reason which exist now."[18] He believes the rise of society to be, like all events, explicable according to mechanical principles. That is to say, the forms of society are determined by "lawful" processes at the level of matter, but there is no logical or moral necessity attached to this or that particular form. Society exists, and existence is taken to be essentially contingent; from the point of view of the mind, the world and society could just as well have been otherwise. In this sense, any order might be taken to be chaotic. Nor are we entitled to say that society or the world might be better or worse were it entirely different. Given the world as it happens to be, the character of society is necessarily as it is. It is merely part of the natural world, and "the close texture of events in nature is what it is by chance; yet what it is by chance determines, according to the occasion offered, what it shall do by nature."[19] For nature, according to Santayana, is just that mechanical order which shows the necessity of what we find in experience.

To a naturalist like Santayana, the Hegelian doctrine of rational determination is egotistical and presumptuous. Reason is *human* reason: while we may find regularities or laws in events, these repetitions are not intrinsically rational and are not efficacious; they are not powers, but the *forms* matter acquires. For forms or "tropes" to be efficacious (and reason itself is such a form) would be magical. Laws are taken to be expressive of the underlying "automatism" of matter. "History goes on in the material world," and the rise and fall of nations and civilizations are ascribed to that world.[20] In this scheme all power is physical, as Santayana persistently contends. Aristocracy, for instance, as he says in *Reason in Society*, "like everything else, has no practical force save that which mechanical causes endow it with."[21] To speak of the power of an idea is to employ a metaphor: "The mind at best vaguely forecasts the result of action"; its premonitions are produced by an unknown mechanism which is the same as that which acts.[22] Politics is fraught with programs and doctrines, but Santayana takes these to be expressions of physical currents, not determinants of events. An idea or an ideal may arise antecedent to action, but an antecedent is not always a cause since the latter, by definition, must be physical. We must look, therefore, for the dynamics of the social process, to the "cosmos" or, as it is called in *Dominations and Powers*, "the generative order of nature." On this strict interpretation of materialism, all that we would wish to call "action" is determined by subterranean forces:

To execute the simplest intention we must rely on fate: our own acts are mysteries to us. Do I know how I open my eyes or how I walk down stairs? Is it the supervising wisdom of consciousness that guides me in these acts? Is it the mind that controls the bewildered body and points out the way to physical habits uncertain of their affinities? Or is it not much rather automatic inward machinery that executes the marvellous work, while the mind catches here and there some glimpse of the operation, now with delight and adhesion, now with impotent rebellion?[23]

Political action, then, is reduced to the status of a process, rather than being an art. Santayana agrees with the behaviorists in taking "the digestion and preparation of action" to be a physical matter.[24] This position of Santayana's is paradoxical, in view of the importance he places on reason and on art. In *Reason in Art* he distinguishes sharply between art and mere automatic process. Art, he says, is "reason propagating itself."[25] It is "that element in the Life of Reason which consists in modifying its environment the better to attain its end."[26] But even here, trying to be a consistent materialist, Santayana is reduced to saying that "arts are not less automatic than instincts."[27] If there is an art of politics, or an art of government, it, too, may only be incidentally rational or artful, and in fact Santayana says that "the Life of Reason is not a power but a result."[28]

Is Santayana denying any significant role to reason? There are inconsistencies in his doctrine of the nature and source of reason which make reason and mind appear impotent, but Santayana nowhere denies the possibility of reason appearing in the world. He terms it "a result." That is, reason is to be achieved; it is not an antecedent condition of human life. This is not to say that his doctrine is free of difficulties. There are many problems in Santayana's metaphysics, some of them serious ones, and of these, a number have troublesome consequences for the doctrine of reason. Democritus, in one of Santayana's *Dialogues in Limbo,* articulates the fatalist implications of an unredeemed materialism: "For what is the truth of the matter? That the atoms in their fatal courses bring all things about by necessity, and that men's thoughts and efforts and tears are but signs and omens of the march of fate, prophetic here, and there deceptive, but always vain and impotent in themselves."[29] If man is thus enslaved to destiny in the guise of matter, we must ask what meaning there may be in the notion of freedom, of art, of reason "modifying its environment." It is hard to see how the life of reason could be anything other than an accidental accord in a meaningless career. Santayana seems to believe that we are saved from meaninglessness and from fatalism by the occasional attainment of rationality.

Epiphenomenalism renders thought impotent even if, in practice, we find it to be significant. If learning is construed as the realization in consciousness of the authoritative factors in the situation in which we must act, then for the epiphenomenalist what we have learned is always really hindsight, since consciousness is only a mirror, wholly ideal and inefficacious. Intelligence, for Santayana, is biological "docility," plasticity, the capacity of instincts to be modified by experience, where experience is understood as undergoing, rather than in its more usual sense for him, awareness. Learning is a process that goes on in the body, in the nervous system, preeminently in the brain. "When this cerebral reorganisation is pertinent to the external situation and renders the man, when he resumes action, more a master of his world, the accompanying thought is said to be practical; for it brings a consciousness of power and an earnest of success."[30] The power, the mastery lie not in the knowledge, but in the organism thus raised to consciousness. Could we say, then, that awareness, knowledge, contributes anything to action? Or is it only something "superadded," a benefit in itself, perhaps, but useless and helpless? To adopt the latter view is to accept a drastic limitation on the possibility of rational conduct: ". . . human will, not controlling its basis, cannot possibly control its effects. Its existence and its efforts have at best the value of a good omen. They show in what direction natural forces are moving in so far as they are embodied in given men."[31] It is doubtful whether Santayana ever provides the metaphysical or epistemological justification for a more optimistic assessment of the power of reason.

NOTES

[1] *DP*, p. 164.

[2] *DP*, p. 5.

[3] "Apologia Pro Mente Sua," in *Philosophy*, p. 507.

[4] *STT*, p. 46.

[5] *RSci*, p. 167.

[6] *Ibid.*, pp. 9–10.

[7] *Scepticism and Animal Faith* (New York: Charles Scribner's Sons, 1923; reprint: New York: Dover Publications, Inc., 1955), p. 47. Hereafter cited as *SAF*.

[8] Cf. *RSci*, pp. 39ff.

[9] "Apologia Pro Mente Sua," in *Philosophy*, p. 520.

[10] *RSci*, p. 47.

[11] *Ibid.*, p. 301.

[12] *RSci*, p. 41.

[13] *DP*, pp. 3–4.

[14] *Reason in Society* (New York: Charles Scribner's Sons, 1905), p. 137. Hereafter cited as *RSoc*.

[15] *DP*, p. 4.

[16] *Ibid.*, p. 295.

[17] Cf. Alcibiades in "Normal Madness," *Dialogues in Limbo* (New York: Charles Scribner's Sons, 1926; reprint: Ann Arbor, Michigan: The University of Michigan Press, Ann Arbor Books), p. 55. Hereafter cited as *DL*.

[18] *Reason in Common Sense* (New York: Charles Scribner's Sons, 1905; second edition, London: Constable and Co. Ltd., 1922), p. 36. Hereafter cited as *RCS*.

[19] *DP*, p. 54.

[20] *Ibid.*, p. 4. For critical comment on the question of the efficacy of form, see pp. 25–26 below.

[21] *RSoc*, p. 111.

[22] *RCS*, p. 214.

[23] *Ibid.*

[24] *Platonism and the Spiritual Life* (London: Constable and Co., 1927; reprint: *Winds of Doctrine* and *Platonism and the Spiritual Life*, New York: Harper Torchbooks, 1957), p. 267. Hereafter cited as *PSL*.

[25] *Reason in Art* (New York: Charles Scribner's Sons, 1905; second edition, London: Constable and Co. Ltd., 1922), p. 13. Hereafter cited as *RA*.

[26] *Ibid.*, pp. 16–17.

[27] *Ibid.*, p. 4.

[28] *RCS*, p. 6.

[29] *DL*, p. 68.

[30] *RCS*, p. 210.

[31] *Ibid.*, p. 215.

CHAPTER 3

The Ambiguities of Santayana's Materialism

SANTAYANA CLAIMS that his philosophy of society, which he characterizes as materialist, must be read in the context of his philosophy of nature. It
is therefore pertinent to ask whether his metaphysics actually supports a
materialist doctrine, or whether we do not have to concede Dewey's point
that Santayana's naturalism is crippled.[1] It has been contended by some critics that whereas his earlier philosophy, resting upon a greater confidence in
man's ability to perceive the mechanical structure of nature, was fundamentally naturalistic, his later view, grounded on "animal faith" in the existence
of the realm of matter, necessitated an abandonment of materialism. I
believe (1) that Santayana was a naturalist and a materialist in the same
sense and on the same grounds throughout; (2) that despite even radical
changes in terminology his "later" ontology is a development of, and not
inconsistent with, his "earlier" philosophy; and (3) that, nevertheless, from
the start his materialism was touched with ambiguity. The insecurity of his
materialism stems from Santayana's perpetual "oscillation," as he calls it,
between transcendentalism and common sense, between scepticism and
animal faith. This results in confusion between statements concerning conscious experience and statements about existence outside awareness.

In the preface to the second edition of *The Life of Reason* Santayana discusses his use in that work of the word "nature"; he points out that it may
have two meanings: existing nature and the idea of nature. Statements applicable to one do not apply to the other, but certain passages are ambiguous as
to their referent. For instance:

I find myself saying (Vol. I, page 125) that "nature is drawn like a sponge, heavy and
dripping from the waters of sentience." Obviously the "nature" in question is the
idea of nature, vague, at first and overloaded with myth, then growing distinct, constant, articulate. Existing nature could not be drawn either soaking or dry from the
waters of sentience: for existing nature is a system of bodies long antedating
sentience. . . .[2]

The ambiguity in Santayana's use of the term "nature" and of the associated terms "the material world," "existence," "reality" is pervasive and, I think, reflects more than literary carelessness. It is epitomized in *Realms of Being* by a confusion in the term "matter."[3]

It would seem that Santayana's temptation to say that nature is drawn from sentience results from his conviction that the existence of the material world is not something encountered, but is inferred from "given" experience. "Experience" in *The Life of Reason* and elsewhere is frequently used to mean *conscious* experience; *crude* experience is the stream of awareness which, thanks to its (imputed) origin in a plastic and impulsive animal, is cumulative and may be reflected upon. Crude experience is, in a sense, experience of objects, but these objects may not be said actually to exist; they are *terms,* interpretations of experience, and are, to use Santayana's word, "ideal." The immediate, "the flux of experience," is "uninterpreted feeling."[4] In *Reason in Common Sense* the immediate is said to exist. In later works such as *Scepticism and Animal Faith* (the preface to *Realms of Being*), however, "nothing given exists" and "existence" is the term applied exclusively to *matter.*[5] But in both *The Life of Reason* and *Realms of Being* the existence of matter, which Santayana insists underlies conscious immediacy, seems really to be an article of faith.

In the first place he makes clear that we do not *perceive* existents directly. In this sense Santayana is a subjectivist even though his criticism of "egotism" in philosophy condemns subjectivism. "Consciousness," he says, "is a born hermit."[6] Perception "is in fact no primary phase of consciousness; it is an ulterior practical function acquired by a dream which has become symbolic of its conditions, and therefore relevant to its own destiny."[7] Nor is the attribution of a dreamlike character to awareness a poetic phrase. The objects of consciousness, being ideal, are imaginary, and their relations to one another are only "dialectical." They would never take on functional significance or symbolic value were it not for the fact that they arise as a result of supposed bodily instincts and needs, marking the eruption of the latter into consciousness and the subsequent awareness of their satisfaction. In themselves objects are images, essences, "forms of imagination."[8] Santayana asserts that "the substance of experience lies in imagination, not in perception, . . . while knowledge and reason are but its chastened and ultimate forms."[9] Chastened but, it would seem, fictional.

In *Reason in Common Sense* Santayana exposes what he considers the ambiguity in Kant's philosophy.[10] Kant was correct, he says, in taking experience to be the substance or matter of nature. Nature, Santayana contends here, is the whole of what could possibly be experienced, and is therefore the cause of that segment of it which is present to us. The cause, that is, in the

only intelligible sense of causation, which Kant himself articulated. But Kant
went on to speak of "conditions" of experience, using that term in a "mystical" sense to mean something efficacious but unknowable that causes nature
itself; i.e., that causes experience in some other and unintelligible sense of
"cause." But being truly unknowable, Santayana says, things-in-themselves
are myths; and being hypostatizations of logical categories, the so-called
transcendental conditions of experience are equally fabulous and equally
illegitimate. Both are inferences from experience to something non-empiri-
cal. He contends that the "subjective" conditions of experience are, in fact,
those characteristics which belong to experience *as* experience and are therefore within experience, not transcendental. And what can be inferred from
experience is not a "metaphysical" or non-natural thing-in-itself, but only
something conceivably experienceable. Experience, then, is just given: it is
uncaused since all causes are discoverable or inferable within it. *Nature* is
"the sum total of its own conditions." *The mind* is *part of* nature; its cause
must lie within nature. "To say it is its own condition or that of other objects
is a grotesque falsehood."[11] But "conditions" of experience, Santayana
asserts, like all causes, must be inferred from experience itself and can only
be empirical. Nature, "the single nature or set of conditions for experience
which the intellect constructs, is the object of our own thoughts and perceptions ideally completed" and is therefore "secondary" like all causes, objects,
conditions, and ideals—all terms, all the interpretants of brute data.[12] At this
point he claims that such a doctrine ought to have been the conclusion of
Kant's critique. But Santayana is as ambiguous and contradictory as he saw
Kant to be. The nominalist and pragmatist strand in his philosophy, observable in his criticism of Kant, is, I think, incoherent with his materialism.

Nature, defined as Santayana says Kant should consistently have defined
it, is not essentially different from the objects conceived to exist within it, but
comprehends them all. According to Santayana, an object or thing is by definition an ideal object, "an imagined potentiality that holds together the epi-
sodes which are actual in consciousness."[13] He takes Kant's faith in
noumenal reality to be unjustified and mystical. Kant would have been correct had he claimed simply that we can have faith in experience itself. What
criticism can teach us is that intellectual knowledge is "practical" even
though hypothetical, and that inferred knowledge is not total ignorance.
Santayana considers the concepts of both common sense and science to be
derivative and hypothetical, but nonetheless verifiable. By "verifiable" he
seems to mean "confirmable by further experience." Our ideas of material
objects and of atoms, of persons and of electric charges are all bridges leading
from one experience to another: "The terms or goals of thought have for
their function to subtend long tracts of sensuous experience, to be ideal links

between fact and fact, invisible wires behind the scene, threads along which inference may run in making phenomena intelligible and controllable."[14]

But Santayana does claim that our experience yields valid, if not actually veridical, knowledge of the nature that exists outside and antecedent to sentience (the physical world), and nature in this sense (the sense in which he commonly conceives it) is not the object of any possible experience. Thought, on his assumptions, cannot contain the physical world that spawns it. Experience and feeling, he explicitly states, are "the only given existence, from which the material part of nature, something essentially dynamic and potential, must be intelligently inferred."[15] This inference is provisional, instrumental: "The addition of a physical substratum to all thinking is only a scientific expedient, a hypothesis expressing the fact that nature is mechanically intelligible even beyond the reaches of minute verification."[16] It is questionable, however, whether the apparatus Santayana provides permits us even to talk about material nature apart from the experience he repeatedly asserts it to generate.

Within experience, he says, we distinguish mind and body in close connection with one another: "The body is an instrument, the mind its function."[17] But by distinguishing them, he shows that we make this connection unintelligible and thus create a philosophic problem. By conceiving the body as distinct from consciousness we make it something which has no logical connection with consciousness or mind. In a passage which is interesting partly because it illustrates the way in which he confuses talk about terms and talk about the referents of those terms, Santayana develops the metaphysical implications of this distinction:

If we isolate the terms mind and body and study the inward implications of each apart, we shall never discover the other. That matter cannot, by transposition of its particles, *become* what we call consciousness, is an admitted truth; that mind cannot *become* its own occasions or determine its own march, though it be a truth not recognized by all philosophers, is in itself no less obvious. Matter, dialectically studied, makes consciousness seem a superfluous and unaccountable addendum; mind, studied in the same way makes nature an embarrassing idea. . . .[18]

Even in the face of his exposure of this bifurcation and its consequences Santayana does not seem to have reached a satisfactory understanding of the relation of mind and body. On his view we are always aware of the content of consciousness, the flux of feeling, not of its natural conditions, i.e., not of the body. Reflection on experience, he claims, leads us to infer the dependence of consciousness on bodily life. Now the body on which consciousness depends could not be the object of consciousness, for that would be for him an idea, a term, and would require a physical substratum. But if the source of consciousness is a body that is inferred, it would still have to be empirical, by Santayana's own statement, and would be no less ideal. He assigns an important place to "Will" in determining consciousness. But the heart of the problem is that for him Will ("psyche" in Aristotle's root sense of the principle of life and movement in an organism as opposed to "spirit" or conscious mind), too, is physical, and must be inferred from the content of consciousness. Its existence is thus in doubt, and we find the Kantian problem of the conditions of consciousness recurring in Santayana's own philosophy.

Whether in science or in common sense, action coupled with further reflection either confirms or forces us to modify or reject our hypotheses. By this means, Santayana maintains, knowledge can still be true of existence. "The abstractions of science," he says, "are extractions of truths." Although "truths cannot of themselves constitute existence with its irrational concentration in time, place, and person, its hopeless flux, and its vital exuberance," he insists that "they can be true of existence; they can disclose that structure by which its parts cohere materially."[19] The concept of matter underlying consciousness is such an abstraction. But embedded in Santayana's statement about science is exactly the kind of ambiguity he sees in Kant's philosophy and in his own discussions of nature cited above; and the ambiguity is more fundamental and more dangerous than he seems to think. For if the existence of which science is said to be true is inferred, it cannot exist outside experience; but if it is not an object of possible experience, it must really be uninferable. Dewey, making this point, says that the conditions underlying experience are, according to Santayana, "humanly unknowable." "But in that case," Dewey asks, "why refer to the underlying conditions as biological?"[20] It is not clear that Santayana believes science to be applicable to anything beyond actual and potential experience. Almost immediately preceding the statement that science discloses the structure of *existence* is the sentence, "Science thus articulates *experience* and reveals its skeleton."[21] The hesitation implicit in these contradictory formulations seems to reflect uncertainty about the actual referent of "existence."

Santayana could be construed to mean that we only have knowledge of the content of experience, but he emphatically (and consistently) denies the "transcendentalist" assertion "that what is inferred exists only in the fooled mind that infers it."[22] He insists repeatedly that we must have faith in the inference from experience. Over and above this he claims that we cannot rest with subjectivism because the very notion of subjectivity presupposes that of objectivity.[23] Despite all his proofs to the contrary, he intends a transcendental critique to lead, not to absolute idealism, but to materialism: "It is quite true that the flux, as it exists in men, is largely psychic; but only because the events it contains are effects of material causes and the images in it are flying shadows cast by solid external things."[24] But given his presuppositions, it does not seem possible that the existence of anything outside experience can be legitimately postulated. "Physical nature," if it is anything at all, must be an undefined term. Santayana's confidence in anything beyond the stream of awareness seems to be a priori.

Much of *Reason in Common Sense* is concerned with the genesis of our *idea* of existence out of the raw material of experience."Nature,""reality," "the material world," which are phenomenologically explicated, are terms in discourse, "personages" of "ideal society" as he puts it in *Reason in Society,* having their locus in consciousness. But many of his statements make claims for "external" reality that are self-contradictory or inconsistent with his conception of the flux of consciousness. To illustrate, "external objects are thought to be principles and sources of experience; they are accordingly conceived realities on an ideal plane."[25] For a materialist the *source* of experience is the physical world. Conceived realities could not be sources of experience and could not, in any case, be actual material existents, much as he wished to retain the latter in his system. *Ideas* of external objects could be principles—but how could they be material? In fact, Santayana claims that we construct ideas of objects, as well as ideas of forms or essences, employing them as norms in regulating the "chaotic" flow of experience: "We attribute independence to things in order to normalise their recurrence. We attribute essences to them in order to normalise their manifestations or constitution. Independence will ultimately turn out to be an assumed constancy in material processes, essence an assumed constancy in ideal meanings or points of reference in discourse."[26]

By posting material processes, "something dynamic and independent," as the cause of perceived recurrences, Santayana says, we lay the basis for mechanical science. The idea of a systematic universe which is the setting for man and society is built of constructs and is similarly normative; the principle that all possible experience must occur in a systematic spatiotemporal universe is not primitive, but a hypothetical inference. "Reality" and "appearance" in this scheme are, respectively, names for regulative concepts and sensations, linked as type and token:

A reality is a term of discourse based on a psychic complex of memories, associations, and expectations, but constituted in its ideal independence by the assertive energy of thought. An appearance is a passing sensation, recognised as belonging to that group of which the object itself is the ideal representative, and accordingly regarded as a manifestation of that object.[27]

The concept of a permanent, independent world, according to Santayana, is an idea framed by intelligence to account for "the cohesion in space and the recurrence in time of recognizable groups of sensations."[28] He takes the necessity of such an idea to be proved by pointing to the "coherence and recurrence in external phenomena."[29] But the "coherence and recurrence in external phenomena" by which the idea of reality is justified is one and the same with that which Santayana invokes it to explain—the coherence and recurrence discovered in an otherwise incoherent stream of consciousness, with irrelevant incoherence discounted. Reality is identified with the idea of reality; the "external objects" which justify the notion of an independent and permanent world are either perceptual regularities or ideal terms, themselves requiring justification. It is plain that Santayana is not able to reach external existence from the vantage point of his epistemology and equally plain that he acknowledged as early as *Reason in Common Sense* that belief in the existence of matter rests on what he later came to call "animal faith." The following is, I believe, important enough to be reproduced here in full:

Let the reader meditate for a moment upon the following point: to know reality is, in a way, an impossible pretension, because knowledge means significant representation, discourse about an existence not contained in the knowing thought, and different in duration or locus from the ideas which represent it. But if knowledge does not possess its object how can it intend it? And if knowledge possesses its object, how can it be knowledge or have any practical, prophetic, or retrospective value? Consciousness is not knowledge unless it indicates or signifies what actually it is not. This transcendence is what gives knowledge its cognitive and useful essence, its transitive function and validity. In knowledge, therefore, there must be some such thing as a justified illusion, an irrational pretension by chance fulfilled, a chance shot hitting the mark.[30]

Santayana admits that to reach "reality" requires knowledge to somehow transcend conscious immediacy, a transcendence he characterizes as "miraculous" and describes dramatically as "a leap out of solipsism" prompted not by reason, but by need, though he claims this leap to be "rationally" justified.[31] The paradigm of transcendence is the inference that other minds exist. But he has the same difficulty in establishing the existence of material objects as he does in proving that of other minds, and in the end succeeds only in making distinctions among ideas.

One of the most penetrating of Santayana's critics, Milton K. Munitz, while acknowledging other undercurrents in Santayana's earlier work, still sees in *The Life of Reason,* along with naturalism in metaphysics and humanism in moral philosophy, a realistic methodology in the theory of knowledge.[32] According to Munitz, Santayana in that work recognizes science as "an elaborately controlled operation that develops out of and has its original basis in common sense."[33] In contrast, he takes Santayana's "later" epistemology, in the form in which it is presented in *Scepticism and Animal Faith,* to result in the sceptical dissolution of science, where the pursuit of science is sanctioned "for practical reasons" but the epistemological theory "proclaims nevertheless its ultimately fictional character."[34] I agree with this judgment, but would add that in both *Reason and Common Sense* and *Reason in Science* common sense itself, where it is analyzed in detail, turns out to be ultimately fictional. That statements which might refute this position may be found in the text is undeniable, but I would say that the seeds of scepticism have already borne fruit in the earlier works.

At the same time, in representing an adjustment to actual existence, whatever that may be, on the part of an individual located in the actual world, Santayana believes knowledge to be representative and relevant. It is representative of that adjustment and of the knower and relevant to, though it may never duplicate, the circumstances to which he may relate. In *Reason in Common Sense,* thought is taken to be an expression of "natural relations" and will to represent "natural affinities."[35] As he worded it a few years later in the paper "Literal and Symbolic Knowledge," "knowledge of nature is a great allegory, of which action is the interpreter."[36] Science and social science, physics and metaphysics, like common sense, are elaborate metaphors which may be more or less adequate but never strictly true. The doctrine of materialism itself is therefore a hypothesis, although he insists that it is a necessary hypothesis and is justified by practice. But as a doctrine, as part of discourse, it must also be justified "dialectically" by its "ideal relations" to other doctrines and concepts, in particular its ground in the concept of matter. And it may be questioned whether Santayana's materialism is adequately supported by his discussions of this concept.

Another critic, William Ray Dennes, grants the continuity between Santayana's earlier and later works but insists that there is a contradiction between his empiricism and his materialism.[37] Beyond this he asks whether Santayana's statement of the materialist principle is not empty. In *Realms of Being* Santayana stipulates that the term "existence" is properly used only to refer to "matter." Dennes asserts that, if by "matter" is meant whatever exists, then saying that only matter exists is meaningless save as a statement of a resolve to use the words "matter" and "material" in a particular way. As a result, Dennes charges, "Santayana's consistently maintained philosophical position does in fact lack any specific and positive content—adds no beliefs about existence and the ways and history of nature to the hypotheses of the sciences and to those beliefs of common sense which are their soil and seed."[38]

It is true that in *The Realm of Matter* Santayana states, "Matter is properly a name for the actual substance of the natural world, whatever that substance may be."[39] This and similar statements seem to justify the charge that his materialism is meaningless. But there is the same ambiguity in the term "matter" as there is in "nature." If we understand what Santayana means by "matter" in this context, the charge might be refuted. Professor Dennes calls attention in the same paper to the confusion generated by failing to distinguish between categories understood as terms and the traits of existence which categoreal terms name. Santayana failed, on occasion, to make this distinction, and it is easy to overlook it in reading his works. When we read in *Realms of Being* that "matter" is a name for the actual substance of the natural world, we must not forget the adjective "properly." *Properly* speaking, matter is existing matter, not Santayana's category. "By the word matter I do not understand any human idea of matter. . . ."[40] All he can say about matter itself is that "it is the principle of existence: it is all things in their potentiality and therefore the condition of their excellence or possible perfection."[41] In *Dominations and Powers* there is a more succinct statement of the same point: "Matter is whatsoever in nature, by its motions and tensions, causes all events to take place and all appearances to appear."[42] Even this is not an empty doctrine since it denies the fundamental tenet of idealism. It is, of course, possible to claim that both doctrines are empty and therefore identical. If they are reducible to statements that "everything is matter (mind)," this is undeniably the case. Santayana takes these to be mutually exclusive propositions, and to a large extent his philosophy is a refutation of idealism. His basic assumptions concerning existence are that it is material and contingent and that mind and reason are products of material forces. But the bare statement of the materialist doctrine does no more than name the principle of existence and does not justify any further characterization of matter. Santayana's materialist philosophy goes much further. It includes a mechanist causal theory, the doctrine known as epiphenomenalism, and what he calls moral naturalism. Each of these plays an important part in his social and political thought.

Now if matter is by definition all existence, then all existence is material, but so far we know nothing more about it. As Professor Dennes points out, Santayana is not making the claim that matter is all there is. He distinguishes between "existence" and "being," or "reality," and between "existence" and "actuality," or presence in consciousness. The realm of matter is only one of the realms of being, each of which has a genuine ontological status. To be a materialist means, to him, not to hold that matter is everything and everything is matter, but that only matter is efficacious in the world. He acknowledges that matter without form could not exist or be efficacious. Now the *way* anything affects anything else, the kind of efficacy it has, is a function of its character, its form. It would seem, then, that form has a kind of efficacy. We could take Santayana to be asserting the weaker claim that form apart from matter has no efficacy, and this does seem to be his thesis. He is saying that essences are not powers; neither are ideas or ideals, which are reflections or translations or emanations or products of the powers of nature. He maintains "that matter is the only *substance, power,* or *agency* in the universe: and this, not that matter is the only *reality,* is the first principle of materialism."[43]

But is it not *formed* matter that is efficacious? What does it mean to strip essences (forms) of power when without form, matter could neither exist nor be efficacious, and could in no way be differentiated or discriminated? And how can matter alone be taken to be the source of all that exists and is valuable? What justification is there for assigning the kind of primacy which Santayana assigns to the realm of matter? Matter, according to him, is the source of all that comes to pass. We owe to it the respect due to God. *"Reverence,"* Santayana says, is due "to power, to the roots and the moral supports of existence; it is therefore due really to the realm of matter only," not to "ideal objects."[44] Piety, for Santayana, is civilized man's obeisance to power imaginatively personified. In politics, as in technology, respect for power must take the form of acquiescence to the authority of existing forces and real needs, rather than subservience to attractive ends wistfully contemplated. This principle is the central thesis of *Dominations and Powers* and the key to Santayana's philosophy of politics.

Even if we define matter as power or substance, we can go no further in its description since, according to Santayana, it is essentially unknowable. Being "sensuous and pictorial," "all human notions of matter, even if not positively fabulous, must be wholly inadequate."[45] For, as Berkeley asked, how can that which is passive resemble that which is active? If this is the case, we can predicate nothing of matter. We are justified in worshipping it but do not know what it is that we obey. Matter itself, if by this term we mean existing matter, is inscrutable. We cannot attribute intelligible properties to it since intelligibility belongs only to the elements of discourse. And Santayana holds discourse to be addressed to ideal essences, to poetic or logical terms. Intrinsically, discourse is manipulation of these terms and is, at its best, playful and inherently rewarding. "When fortune or necessity diverts our attention from this congenial ideal sport to crude facts and pressing issues, we turn our frail poetic ideas into symbols for those terrible irruptive things. In that paper money of our own stamping, the legal tender of the mind, we are obliged to reckon all movements and values of the world."[46] If we could talk of existing matter at all, it could only be to attribute causal efficacy to it—since nothing "ideal" is efficacious and "matter is the name for that which is"—and to deny it rationality on the grounds that rationality is defined by and belongs to discourse. Matter, if that word names anything, must be potent, but it cannot be subsumed under rational categories. A doctrine based on it would indeed be empty, but no doctrine can be so based. It cannot be matter per se that satisfies Santayana's materialist thesis, but a term which is symbolic of actual power and susceptible of interpretation and analysis. Santayana's conception of knowledge and science is nominalistic even in his "earlier" works. Both religion and science, he says, "live in imaginative discourse, one being an aspiration and the other a hypothesis."[47] Yet he distinguishes "dialectical" or formal science from physics on the grounds that the "ultimate" object of science is *not* ideal.[48] I believe him to mean that physics is factual. Its termini are independent "objects"; those of mathematics and logic are essences. But there remains the problem cited above concerning the doctrines of "objects," of "reality," and of "facts." At best Santayana's materialism might be understood as an instrumental hypothesis enabling us to cope with the invisible forces that run the world. As such, it need not be veridical. But at important points the phraseology in which it is stated is indeed contradictory.

In its significance for his political philosophy perhaps the most important property of the existing world is what Santayana believes to be its mechanical and "automatic" operation. In *The Life of Reason* the principle of mechanism is invoked to account for the regularities we discover in experience. Mechanism is postulated to govern a "cosmos" which, it is claimed, underlies consciousness, or at least must be taken to do so for practical purposes. The mechanical order is one of natural necessity. Although the distinction of chaos and order is relative, "a cosmos does not mean a disorder with which somebody happens to be well pleased; it means a necessity from which everyone must draw his happiness." Efficacy is defined by Santayana as mechanical: "For to be efficacious a principle must apply necessarily and proportionately. . . ."[49] According to Santayana's epiphenomenalist interpretation, a *principle,* being an idea, should, of course, have no power or efficacy. "Efficacy" here must be interpreted to mean "validity." Were he speaking of causes, Santayana would have had to use other language, and even were he to do so, the meaning of "efficacy" would be questionable, since, as has been pointed out, causes, like principles, are in his system secondary and ideal.

"The cosmos," like "nature" and "matter," is an ambiguous term. Mechanism, its principle, is called "the dialectic of the irrational." Existence itself is said to be irrational and change unintelligible, yet "the total flux is continuous and naturally intelligible."[50] The contradiction might be resolved by interpreting "the cosmos" not as existing reality, but as a construct or model which we elaborate to satisfy practical and intellectual needs. There are grounds for this interpretation. Santayana asserts that by "the natural

world," in which he locates the conditions of consciousness and in reference
to which he says consciousness and purpose can attain practical efficacy, he
means "simply the world constructed by categories found to yield a constant,
sufficient, and consistent object."[51] Explanation belongs to the realm of discourse; we must be careful to limit its scope to that which is intelligible. And
for Santayana the intelligible would be the world we *think* underlies experience, not the mysterious potency which, he claims, actually does give rise to
experience. In Santayana's system mechanism is an explanatory principle; it
does not have to, nor could it, apply, except symbolically, to existing matter.
Conversely, I would suggest that it is possible to elaborate a complex and
significant materialism without denying that matter is literally unknowable.
In Santayana's system such knowledge as we can have is "faith mediated by
symbols."[52]

In *Dominations and Powers* Santayana reaffirms and elaborates the thesis
that social causation is physical; physical causes, he claims, are "movements
generating one event continuously out of another" and not merely mental
associations. "There is," he further states, "an uninterrupted flux of measurable and traceable events, a transformation of the same objects rather than an
association of independent images."[53] "The same object" might be ideally
fixated. But if the flux of matter is unintelligible and irrational, it cannot be
composed of "measurable and traceable events." "Physical causes" so
defined must be conceptual, not existential. And if this is the case, how can
they be powers? And how can they be said to exist outside a mind? The solu-
tion can only be that, according to Santayana, what we conceive as causes are
symbols of underlying efficacy. The symbolic model is ordered according to
mechanistic principles indicating, but never truly portraying, an order
beneath. Intelligibility is a property of ideas; logical necessity is not applicable to existence. Yet to explain an event is, paradoxically, to make its occurrence, its existence, intelligible. If the universe were completely chaotic, no
explanation would be possible. We must therefore minimally assume certain
"habits in matter" underlying the regularities we perceive or infer in experience. To speak of causes is to construct an order or schema into which events
(strictly our ideas of events) are fitted. Such an order must be mechanical:
were it not, were causes imperfectly "efficacious," we could not venture to
explain. Thus, as Democritus perceived, "mechanism is not one principle of
explanation among others. In natural philosophy, where to explain means to
discover origins, transmutations, and laws, mechanism is explanation
itself."[54]

Science represents the practical effort of a conscious organism to dominate
existence by understanding its own conditions. Understanding consists in
seeing the repeated and repeatable forms of experience to be manifestations

of regular, automatic processes. Yet, says Santayana, materialism, when properly understood, is not an inhuman doctrine. It loses its sting partly because it does not reduce the ideal to the material and partly, too, because the automatic and mechanical properties attributed to matter are only symbolic. The world is not reduced to mechanical simplicity nor is man. In the end Santayana leaves room in his system for the mystery of existence: matter itself is not a conceptual model like the atoms of science. It is "a primeval plastic substance of unknown potentiality, perpetually taking on new forms." But on his view these forms which matter acquires are not in themselves potent or efficacious; they "are all passive and precarious, while the plastic stress of matter is alone creative and, as far as we can surmise, indestructible."[55] It is only forms that appear in experience. As Bertrand Russell points out, there is an unbridgeable gulf in Santayana's system between essence and matter.[56] There is such a gap also between experience and its supposed material conditions, with the important consequence that Santayana is unable satisfactorily to justify his materialism. Dewey sees "two movements and two positions in Santayana, which are juxtaposed, but which never touch."[57] Such are his naturalism and the psychological empiricism to which he adheres despite his own sharp criticism.

In the last analysis the core of Santayana's naturalism does not lie in his posit of an unknowable substratum, but in his belief in the fruitfulness of nature and in his doctrine of the naturalness of mental and cultural life and of all legitimate ideals. Its justification must rest in its details and in the conclusions to which it leads him; his social and political philosophy may be considered as a case in point. As for his theory of knowledge, perhaps we may apply to it the comment he makes regarding the theory of knowledge associated with German philosophy: "This theory of knowledge is a tangle of equivocations; but even if it were correct it would be something technical, and the technical side of a great philosophy, interesting as it may be in itself, hardly ever determines its essential views."[58]

NOTES

[1] John Dewey, "Half-hearted Naturalism," *The Journal of Philosophy,* XXIV, No. 3 (February 3, 1927), 57–64.

[2] *RCS,* p. viii.

[3] *Realms of Being,* 4 vols.: *The Realm of Essence; The Realm of Matter; The Realm of Truth; The Realm of Spirit* (New York: Charles Scribner's Sons, 1927–40).

[4] *RCS,* p. 41.

[5] Cf. *RCS,* p. 207; *SAF,* p. 42.

[6] *RCS,* p. 48. The concept of egotism will be discussed in Chapter VII below.

[7] *Ibid.,* p. 50.

[8] *Ibid.*

[9] *Ibid.*

[10] *Ibid.,* Chapter IV, "On Some Critics of This Discovery," pp. 84–117.

[11] *Ibid.,* pp. 103–4.

[12] *Ibid.,* pp. 105–6.

[13] *Ibid.,* p. 104.

[14] *Ibid.,* p. 77. Cf. also: "To substitute faith for knowledge might mean to teach the intellect humility, to make it aware of its theoretic and transitive function as a faculty for hypothesis and rational fiction, building a bridge of methodical inferences and ideal unities between fact and fact, between endeavor and satisfaction." *Ibid.,* p. 94.

[15] *Ibid.,* p. 104. The ambiguity in Santayana's concept of nature is revealed by the fact that the material, in some contexts identified with nature, is here said to be "part of nature."

[16] *Ibid.,* p. 210.

[17] *Ibid.,* p. 206.

[18] *Ibid.*

[19] *RSci,* pp. 72–73.

[20] John Dewey, *op. cit.,* p. 62.

[21] *RSci,* p. 72, italics added.

[22] *Ibid.,* p. 313.

[23] *RCS,* p. 316.

[24] *Ibid.*

[25] *Ibid.,* p. 77.

[26] *Ibid.,* p. 74.

[27] *Ibid.,* p. 82.

[28] *Ibid.,* pp. 82–83.

[29] *Ibid.,* p. 83.

[30] *Ibid.,* pp. 150–51.

[31] *Ibid.,* p. 151.

[32] "Ideals and Essences in Santayana's Philosophy," in *Philosophy,* pp. 183–215.

[33] *Ibid.,* p. 188.

[34] *Ibid.,* p. 190.

[35] Cf. *RCS,* p. 221.

[36] In Justus Buchler and Benjamin Schwartz, eds., *Obiter Scripta: Lectures, Essays and Reviews* (New York: Charles Scribner's Sons, 1936), pp.

108–50; passage cited, p. 140. Hereafter cited as *OS.*

[37] "Santayana's Materialism," in *Philosophy,* pp. 417–43.

[38] *Ibid.,* p. 423.

[39] (Charles Scribner's Sons, 1930), p. 140. Hereafter cited as *RM.*

[40] *Ibid.*

[41] *Ibid.,* p. v.

[42] *DP,* p. 18.

[43] "Apologia Pro Mente Sua," in *Philosophy,* p. 509.

[44] *RM,* p. xiii.

[45] *Ibid.,* p. viii.

[46] *Character and Opinion in the United States* (New York: Charles Scribner's Sons, 1920; reprint: New York: Doubleday Anchor Books), pp. 103–4.

[47] *RSoc,* p. 201.

[48] *RSci,* p. 78. Santayana employs the adjective "dialectical" in several senses. In its most important meanings for him it refers (1) to a "Socratic" determination of intent, or (2) to formal or logical relations among ideas *as* ideas.

[49] *Ibid.,* pp. 76–77.

[50] *Ibid.,* pp. 77–78.

[51] *RR,* p. 20.

[52] "Apologia Pro Mente Sua," in *Philosophy,* p. 504.

[53] *DP,* p. 148.

[54] *RCS,* p. 17.

[55] *RM,* p. 100.

[56] "The Philosophy of Santayana," in *Philosophy,* pp. 451–74; cf. p. 458.

[57] John Dewey, *op. cit.,* p. 64.

[58] *Egotism in German Philosophy* (New York: Charles Scribner's Sons, 1915; second edition, 1939), p. 21. Hereafter cited as *EGP.*

CHAPTER 4

Natural Society

IN *Reason in Society* Santayana distinguishes three "stages" of society, "the natural, the free, and the ideal."[1] Briefly, "natural society" is the association of individuals for the purposes of nutrition, reproduction, and governance. "Free society" unites people by affinity rather than necessity. And "ideal society" is symbolic, comprising the universe of discourse and the conceived objects of belief and veneration. It would be appropriate to speak of three levels, or, to use a term Santayana occasionally employs, dimensions, rather than three stages of society. Natural, free, and ideal societies coexist in time and are all factors in human history. Whereas free and ideal societies presuppose the existence of natural society, the latter has an ideal counterpart and may at times develop characteristics of free society. And free society has both natural and ideal aspects.

It is the ramifications of natural society which are held to determine the structure of the social order and the character of civilization. The basis of free and ideal society is established in natural society, the function of which is "to produce the individual and to equip him with the prerequisites of moral freedom" and of the life of reason.[2] The thesis of Santayana's materialism is that society is an elaboration of animal life and consequent upon organismic requirements. This doctrine is not one of economic determinism. Political man is biological man; his productivity is contributory to, but not primarily determinative of, the social order. Love and family life, industry, government, and war are equally functions of natural society, and only love is in any sense primary. Animal life is requisite for the rise of spiritual and moral life and must itself be perpetually regenerated. Thus, the reproductive function is said to contain potentially all that human life is capable of realizing and to be generative not simply of a new animal but of the whole range of values.[3] All society, then, is natural in its origins. Granted this, what is the distinctive meaning of the expression "natural society"?

We have already seen that nature, in *The Life of Reason,* is understood both as "the environing reality" and as the representation of that reality in "the notion, universally prevalent among men, of a cosmos in space and time, an animated material engine called nature."[4] The cosmos is conceived to be a physical system, the system of causes. This engine is automatic and mechanical in its operation, nature or matter being governed by natural necessity. Mechanical syndromes tend toward the achievement of distinctive forms, and the flux of existence is pictured as a passage of matter from one form to another. This conception is identical in *The Life of Reason* and *Realms of Being*. In neither is it considered "rational" for any given form to be embodied, and in both the essential property of matter is change. It is conceived as a flux, similar to the flux of consciousness in being always in process, but unlike the latter in being causative rather than epiphenomenal.[5]

The flux of existence is an evolution, not in the Aristotelian sense of generation guided by pre-existing natures, but an accidental, cumulative evolution characterized by occasional variations mechanically caused. Santayana conceives life, human nature, and society to have arisen in this process, their birth in itself constituting a change, a development, but not intrinsically implying any progress. Progress, according to him, is a moral, not a historical, category, determined by consciously entertained goals and not by physical processes. Nature does not really progress, but progress in one respect or another may be defined. A history is only occasionally and incidentally a progress, and the emergence of society is simply part of natural history. Society is natural, then, in the sense that it is not artificial. It is a spontaneous development and not, as the "social contract" theorists would have it, deliberately instituted. The sheer process of its growth is intrinsically irrational and blind. Social institutions in themselves are products of the "mechanical" operation of nature, not of intelligence, purpose, reason, or art. Santayana illustrates this in *Reason in Society* by the genesis of the family and of government. Government is described as being at root nothing but custom codified into law and enforced. As such it represents the inertia of habit rather than the intervention of reason. And to Santayana, habit, which is the beginning of all morality, "is a physical law," an illustration of the tendency of nature to repeat itself rather than to realize new possibilities. "What are called the laws of nature are so many observations made by man on a way things have of repeating themselves by replying always to their old causes, and never, as reason's prejudice would expect, to their new opportunities."[6] It is as "the political representative of a natural equilibrium, of custom, of inertia" that government belongs to natural society. It is simply a mechanical complication in nature. It may turn out to be good or useful, in which case Santayana would call it "rational"; but he says it arises "solely because it is inevitable" and not for the sake of any value it may be seen to have: "it is by no means a representative of reason."[7]

But isn't government or legislation or a change in either of these sometimes instituted purposively in order to achieve some end which is thought to be beneficial? In what sense may such an innovation be said to be representative of custom or inertia or a natural equilibrium? In *Reason in Society* Santayana claims that major social change is unlikely to come from within and more often results from conquest;[8] this is begging the question. In *Dominations and Powers* he classifies social reform as "militant," meaning that it is the product of a counter-current in the course of nature and not intrinsically rational, even if it is thought to be so. His thesis in that book is that if a militant interference with the "natural" course of events is successful, it is so because the underlying forces are already in harmony with it and ready to fall into equilibrium.

Being a product of natural evolution is not sufficient to identify natural society. For example, the family, natural in its origin, may lose its natural status. It ceases to be associated with the pleasures of love or with the "instincts" that relate parents and children or with the benefits derived by each. Then, Santayana says, the family persists as a "political and industrial" unit, which, while it "still thinks itself natural," has become "casual and conventional."[9] Accordingly, it would seem that by "natural society" Santayana means spontaneous or instinctive society: where instinct no longer enforces dependence, an established social relation may be perpetuated and put to other uses, but it is said to be no longer natural. Institutions and customs, being self-perpetuating, conflict with instinct; inertia competes with spontaneous impulse, and society tyrannizes over the vital individual. In contrast, "when man was nearer to the animal and his body and soul were in happier conjunction, when society, too, was more compulsive over the individual, he could lend himself more willingly to being a figure in the general pageant of the world."[10] There is, however, no place among the stated categories of *Reason in Society* for institutions which persist beyond the period in which they are natural and appropriate. The family, hardened into permanence and performing functions for which it may not even be suited, is certainly not a form of free society, for the latter is not in any sense instrumental; Santayana defines "free society" as the mutual cultivation by sympathetic individuals of their very unanimity for its own sake. Nevertheless, he takes care to point out the historical and moral importance of "artificial" institutions. Government, one of his paradigmatic examples of the naturalness of the organs of society, may also become artificial, as has been the case in modern Europe, where the development of democracy and individualism was accompanied by the establishment of "great artificial governments." There "the single man stands alone before an impersonal written law, a constitutional government, and a widely diffused and contagious public opinion, characterised by enormous inertia, incoherence, and blindness."[11] But custom and inertia are constituents of government when it arises naturally, and nature is by definition blind when it generates governments as well as when it gives birth to tornadoes. How then may government be artificial?

Santayana contrasts modern society with a feudal hierarchy: feudal rule retained what he considers to be the instinctive character of the natural family and the tribe. It was still largely a face-to-face relationship and an integral part of personal life. Subsequently, rulers and, eventually, parliaments came to represent, not persons, but great states. The hold such governments have over their subjects is indirect and impersonal. An example of such a government is political democracy: the people who live under it have not created the democratic state, although to some extent they control it. Moreover it is not a product of their needs; "the state administered is a prodigious self-created historical engine," an adventitious and secondary growth like the political family, which persists through inertia and compels involuntary cooperation.[12]

Even if they are political, modern government and the modern family as well, with its superimposed political and economic functions, remain natural not merely in their origins but in the further senses of "natural society" which will be discussed below. But "artificial" and "political" institutions are too important in the history of civilization for their status not to be explicitly recognized. And in his analysis, if not in the brief and inaccurate summary at the end of *Reason in Society*, Santayana may be said to distinguish a fourth stage or level of society, which could appropriately be called "political society." Political societies are civilized societies—states and the social institutions of which they are composed, in which men are indirectly associated through the medium of a fixed relational structure. Plato, Santayana says, has shown "a passage from ideal to political conditions" in describing how a tribe evolves into a state.[13] The state originates when a tribe establishes itself in a territory, outgrows its local resources, and becomes expansionist. Once this occurs, slaves, an army, a bureaucracy, and a corps of professionals are all required to maintain the community in existence. Thus, institutions come to perform the functions originally shared by the members of a family or tribe. And Santayana notes that it is in the course of such expansion that civilization (and war as well) has its inception.

Nature (the realm of causal efficacy), according to Santayana, is a complex of specific powers interacting in ways which may be characterized both mechanically and morally. "All force, implication, or direction inhere in the constitution of specific objects and live in their interplay."[14] Thus, to speak of natural society might be to speak of the interaction of individuals responsible for the history of civilization. Political society, on the other hand, would be the form that interaction assumes when the mechanisms evolved by interdependent and aggressive people for the ordering of their lives and the furtherance of their enterprises become functionally autonomous and ends in themselves.

For Santayana, the adjective "political" has pejorative connotations. In so far as they represent vested interests rather than living need, political institutions are irrational and seem to block the achievement of the life of reason. Yet, Santayana realizes, to the extent that they are functional, institutions may be rational. In becoming entrenched, they generate and satisfy new needs and serve as bases for further development, so that to overthrow a political institution might be to destroy a source of satisfaction and a ground of significant ideals. Most important in this connection is the fact that the political stage of society is the stage of civilization. Santayana denies that this in itself marks an advance in human well-being. He despises romanticism; wealth, safety, variety of experience are not, for him, absolute goods but can only become good as ingredients in a rational life. But he holds in *The Life of Reason* that unless reflection can synthesize "persistent and ideal harmonies" out of the cacophony of competing interests, we are living the life of animals.[15] To live reflectively requires that the basic needs are satisfied and that there be leisure and energy left over for aesthetic enjoyment. Consequently, civilization is necessary for any higher values to be realized. The development of art and intellect requires the increased scope that wealth and diversified activity make possible. Intrinsic to the life of reason is the ability to contemplate and compare many different objects and events. The span of attention must be increased, requiring memory and purpose to take the place of sheer spontaneity. The possibility of turning "instinct and dream" into "a steadfast art of living" lies in transcending immediacy and recognizing more distant relationships.[16] We must remember that for Santayana it would not be that recognition itself which constitutes the life of reason but the relations between need and satisfaction which it reflects.

Political society, like free society, is an outgrowth of natural society. Unlike free society, it is important primarily because of the instrumental functions it performs, but it is not wholly distinct from the free forms of society. Being part of the environment and heritage of every individual in a state, political society has specific significance. The idea of the nation to which an individual belongs is especially revered. This reverence is a constituent of patriotism, itself a form of free society. Patriotism, Santayana says, is both love of country and interest in one's country's welfare—an interest which is inseparable from a commitment to what one believes will enhance that welfare. Such a commitment may, of course, be irrational, but participation in the political life of the nation is now essential to the life of reason. The function of political parties is to unite individuals advocating a single policy, a single conception of the public welfare. Rather than being in conflict with it, party allegiance is an element of patriotism. In *Dominations and Powers* Santayana's assessment of political partisanship is altered, but in *Reason in Society* he asserts firmly that love of country, if it is not just blind and lazy, must involve a demand for change, a policy concerning what kind of change is desirable, and the exertion of effort in the direction of that change.[17]

Natural society is not for Santayana, as it would be for Plato, an ideal to which society would conform if it were perfect. Nor is it natural in the sense that its properties are necessary or unquestionable. Natural society is a form of existing society, imperfect, contingent, and changing, an appropriate subject for historical and scientific investigation and for criticism. Santayana distinguishes natural from free and ideal society on the grounds that the former is always an association of physical individuals or groups thereof; it is essentially face-to-face society. "Natural society unites beings in time and space. . . . In marriage and the family, in industry, government, and war, attention is riveted on temporal existences, on the fortunes of particular bodies, natural or corporate."[18] Ideal society, on the other hand, is wholly immaterial, composed of ideas and ideals, while free society, based on devotion to ideals rather than physical need or instinct, may unite persons far distant in space and time and never physically present to one another. Santayana never denies the existence of "corporate bodies," though he never takes them to be organic individuals. Both natural society and political society are composed of such organizations; families, armies, governments, states have both natural (i.e., causal) and ideal (i.e., cognitive and symbolic) reality. None of these organizations is wholly physical and temporal. Santayana insists upon both the distinction and the relation between the natural and the ideal, the existent and the "perfect" form or essence which it embodies or toward which it "naturally" moves. It is in this relation that value and morality have their origin. "The value of existences is wholly borrowed from their ideality, without direct consideration of their fate, while the existence of ideals is wholly determined by natural forces, without direct relation to their fulfilment."[19]

By "ideal," it must be noted, Santayana variously means: (1) purely formal, being an *essence* or meaning; (2) *mental,* being an *idea*; (3) being an *end* of development or a *goal* consciously entertained, in so far as either an end or a goal is as yet potential. These cannot be added together to constitute a definition of ideality, for they are not altogether compatible. The ideal in all of these senses is "real" but not materially existent; in other respects, however, the senses are all distinct. An essence, by definition, cannot be intrinsically valuable, while an end or goal may. Ideas, according to Santayana, "exist" in a way that neither essences nor ends do (save as these are held "in view" as ideas). The question of the kind of being or reality that essences possess, like that of the status of ideas, is a problem in Santayana's metaphysics which cannot be dealt with here. Another metaphysical problem which can only be mentioned arises in connection with his assertion that potentialities are present actualities.[20] If ends are potentialities and hence actual, in what sense may they said to be ideal?

Society has its foundation in matter—the realm of causation and efficacy—but it rises above the merely causal, ordering itself in terms of transcendent ideals. A pair of individuals becomes a family, a collection of families a clan, a number of tribes a nation: each unit summarized and idealized in a symbol which personifies the whole in the lives of its members. Society never exists without a symbolic dimension, which is not less significant for being ubiquitous. The genesis of society is analogous to and accompanied by that of morality: material and mechanical forces, interacting in highly complex ways, generate persistent drives which are the substance of moral life. Pervasive and compelling needs are directed toward representative satisfactions or *ideals*. A "*moral* ideal" is conceived by Santayana to be a generalized object of striving or aspiration, of respect or affection, of worship or allegiance, all of which rest on interest or need.[21]

Just as everything natural has an ideal—a goal or norm of development, its possible perfection—the biological processes which are the substance of society create interests, ideals, and purposes which reflect the dynamic processes beneath and serve as foci of social order: "Wherever interests and judgments exist, the natural flux has fallen, so to speak, into a vortex, and created a natural good, a cumulative life, and an ideal purpose. Art, science, government, human nature itself, are self-defining and self-preserving: by partly fixing a structure they fix an ideal."[22] Existing society, comprising natural, political, and free society, is made up of conscious individuals aware of these goods and purposes. The powers of nature and society are personified symbolically in awareness, their images constituting what Santayana calls "ideal society." It is these symbols which he believes give meaning to the social process. Thus, social relations are in part ideal, involving images or symbols, however inchoate, to which participating individuals feel some sort of commitment. The ontological status of these ideal figures is unclear. It is as though a number of individuals, standing in different positions, all were to look at a given object, each "seeing" it differently, but at the same time all looking beyond it toward an idealized version or symbol of it which, though not existent, is nevertheless "really real" and the true object of emotional attachment as well as cognition. Thus, different persons experience the social setting differently, and yet all recognize, however dimly, and act so as to express allegiance to, one nation. A person in love directs his affection toward an ideal person who would satisfy his total need. And in loving God a whole society of persons love the symbol of their perfect happiness. These ideals surround and justify social life. The image of the ideal beloved, of love itself, of clan, of country, or of an enterprise such as art or science to which one adheres, all belong to ideal society. God, nature, mankind (which for Santayana *are* our ideas of them), the creatures of the artistic or scientific imagination, comprise a world in which the spirit lives and discovers freedom and immortality. There is profound moral wisdom in this conception. But from an ontological point of view it is problematic. In what does the being of these ideal objects consist? If we could say that their reality is their function in the lives of individuals, we would be consistent with the admittedly pragmatic strain in Santayana's philosophy.[23] But he gives them a special kind of being in a realm of their own. Their universe is ideal society, containing, in addition to moral ideals, all the objects of discourse and of contemplation. It prefigures the realm of essence.

The ideas which populate ideal society are not sensations or perceptions, but constructs—products of intelligence which are based on empirical data (their "material" is said to be "sensuous").[24] Ideas are regulative terms—the "objects," categories, and theories in terms of which the flux of immediacy is ordered and interpreted. They are, therefore, the items which, Santayana says, serve as foci of thought and action. We might characterize their function as that of "final causes" of psychic activity: as Santayana reads Aristotle, a final cause is attractive, but passive (as are Plato's Ideas and Santayana's Essences); the impetus of attraction lies in the power that is attracted to it, rather than in the attractive object. As the Stranger realizes in Santayana's Dialogue "The Secret of Aristotle," " 'Tis love that makes the world go round and not, as idolatrous people imagine, the object of love. The object of love is passive and perhaps imaginary."[25] Recognizing, then, that it is not a power but a projection of a power, we could say an idea is a controlling cause of cognition, or, to use Dewey's term, a dominant quality. Santayana calls it "a goal of thought," "an ideal term of reference and signification by allegiance to which the details of consciousness first become parts of a system and of a thought." Thus, an idea is an ideal or achievement of psychic life, expressing and symbolizing "a functional relation in the diffuse existences to which it gives a name and a rational value."[26]

What does it mean to say that the realm of ideas is a *society?* First, there are the mutual relations of ideas to one another. Secondly, Santayana looks upon symbols as "presences," "personages" in whose company we live; he thereby transforms knowledge and science, as well as art and religion, into mythmaking. The organizing principles of intellectual and practical life are represented by images or formulas, schemata, which are not just discursively significant but also interesting in themselves. By definition, for Santayana, ideas are attractive, are objects of "love." But they seem, in his system, to be irreducibly private. "The lover of representation, be he thinker or dramatist, moves by preference in an ideal society. His communion with the world is half a soliloquy, for the personages in his dialogue are private symbols, and being symbols they stand for what is not themselves."[27]

In thus conceiving ideas to be private, Santayana leaves himself open to the charge of solipsism. He also creates a special problem for his metaphysics of society. "Free society" will be defined as the society of individuals who associate for the sake of ideas and ideals which they share. Shared ideas even provide an associative connection among persons far distant from one another not just in space but in time; Santayana believes we enter into free society with persons long dead, but with whom we share interests. But he does not explain how private symbols can be shared. He believes that similar experiences yield similar forms of consciousness but still holds that these ideas are in strictness not even comparable precisely because they are not shared.[28] Ideal society is mythical, an appearance of society, or better, perhaps, a society of appearances. It can and does represent powers in nature; it is not itself a constellation of powers but of images. In a real sense, however, for Santayana, it is the only society we know because it is only through representatives in ideal society that we know anything at all. But it is "a drama enacted exclusively in the imagination. Its personages are all mythical, beginning with that brave protagonist who calls himself I and speaks all the soliloquies."[29] Even the idea of one's self is a symbolic object, a term, distinguished from other terms only by its position in relation to them. The ideas of other selves are "echoes of those ideal lives in one another," actual presences, but distinct from and inadequately representative of the souls they symbolize.[30] Also members of the mythical company are the notions of country, posterity, humanity, and the gods, each of which is a sign of real forces but, like all symbols, is passive, partial, and perspectival. Nature itself is seen to be part of ideal society, once we recognize that in referring to it we mean "the ideal order of existences in space and time" which is described by science, and not something which we can merely indicate as "All-there-is."[31] Natural society, free and political society, too, in being present to us, are ideal.

Natural society is, in Santayana's terms, a scientific category, indicating, or, more exactly, symbolizing, the causal basis of the social order, the compulsory activities of human animals which insure their survival and determine the tenor of their lives. That these activities may be conventional, in the sense that they might have taken different forms, is not denied. Alternatives to the family, for instance, have been conceived and even practiced. The components of natural society are necessary only in that the absence of any and every form of them would result in physical extinction. Again, performance of any of the functions of love, industry, government, or war may be carried beyond the requirements of necessity and may become an end in itself. This does not mitigate their essentially compulsory character.

The concepts of natural society and of political society into which it develops may be said, therefore, to represent the organization of persons with respect to what sociologists have called "the functional prerequisites of continuous social life."[32] Yet the basis of this organization is not teleological but instinctive; its function in serving these needs is derivative. Natural society involves, of necessity, intimate personal relatedness; because of its biological roots, "instinctive society" is not only the fundamental form of society but also a pervasive determinant of individual character and experience. But society, as will be shown, is not taken by Santayana to be the sole, or even the primary, determinant of character. His emphasis on physical causation leads to a belief in a biological and racial, rather than a societal, personality.

Like everything natural, natural society has moral ramifications. "Every man, every material object, has moral affinities enveloping an indomitable personal nucleus or brute personal kernel."[33] Santayana never abandons the principle that physical nature is the source of value and morality, of purposes and ideals, but "natural society" (which we may, in this connection, take to include political society) refers to the machinery of existing society apart from its moral quality. Santayana holds the moral dimension of nature to lie in the way we interpret what we experience. Moral perception, that is, perception of a natural object as a moral agent or as having moral qualities, like moral judgment, involves an image which he takes to derive from a temporary, personal orientation. Such a picture is a projection of one's own interest or Will, bearing some relation to environing circumstances but not revealing anything of the intrinsic character of that which it is taken to represent. In *Reason in Science* it is stressed that terms expressing value judgments or feelings merely signify transient conditions in a perceiver—his views and intentions. They do not stand for powers or causes in the inferred objects of perception. "Moral unities are created by a point of view, as right and left are, and for that reason are not efficacious."[34] It is therefore inappropriate, Santayana holds, to use moral terms in the context of natural science, natural history, or natural philosophy. They are to be avoided in social philosophy (i.e., in the metaphysics of society), too, as Santayana points out in *Dominations and Powers*, asserting that "the dynamic unity in a society is material only, and its moral unity mythical or verbal."[35]

In the end, any picture of the world is, according to Santayana, a myth; but a moral myth is further divorced from the circumstances which inspired it. Materialism, involving only the logically necessary minimum of interpretation, is the most satisfactory myth: if we abandon it, we must give up not only any attempt to explain phenomena but the very presuppositions we must make in order to participate in everyday life. It is true that Santayana distinguishes between myth and science, on the grounds that (1) science is verifiable, while myth is not, and (2) myth takes its terms to represent actual but unseen existences, whereas scientific terms are discursive instrumentalities, supposing no objects other than those given in perception. On the other hand, Santayana takes both science and myth to be representative of factors in experienced reality, and, if a myth proved valid, it would be ipso facto scientific. Thus, he states, "science might accordingly be called a myth conscious of its essential ideality, reduced to its fighting weight and valued only for its significance."[36]

Belief in the myth of independent and intrinsic moral reality is similarly inescapable and essential to survival. Santayana does not, in distinguishing nature from moral interpretation, deny this but only makes an ontological separation between the two. While its source is organic, morality does not come into being until judgment occurs, until objects and processes are *seen as* good or bad, congenial or hateful. And in so far as it is something seen, as it is an element in consciousness, the moral quality of anything is fictional. Natural society per se is non-moral, yet it has a moral life because its members are conscious of their goals and of the mutual relevance of their acts. Nature is moralized and rationalized by mind: "Nature's works first acquire a meaning in the commentaries they provoke; mechanical processes have interesting climaxes only from the point of view of the life that expresses them, in which their ebb and flow grows impassioned and vehement."[37] Events, on the other hand, are taken to be mechanical and to flow imperceptibly into one another. Ends—termini as well as goals—like successes and failures, are imputed to nature. They are not discovered in nature or even in crude experience; experience is organized and divided into periods only as a consequence of the effort to control circumstances in the interest of some impulse, drive, or need. This effort inspires reflection, and in reflection the flux of awareness is conceptually arrested and morally ordered.

"Society exists," says Santayana, "so far as does analogous existence and community of ends."[38] So defined, society involves the possession by individuals of a common heritage and similar circumstances (but not necessarily physical or temporal proximity) and shared goals. Society of this sort may exist "invisibly."[39] Furthermore, if society is defined in this way it is not compulsory: it is not a necessary part of the system of production and reproduction whereby the race is perpetuated. Thus, the definition does not apply to natural society. The society of individuals who associate voluntarily, perhaps accidentally, for the sake of ideals they hold in common, and who are enabled to do so because of their similar histories and parallel situations is *free* society: "Whatever spirit in the past or future, or in the remotest regions of the sky shares our love and pursuit, say of mathematics or of music, or of any ideal object, becomes, if we can somehow divine his existence, a partner in our joys and sorrows, and a welcome friend."[40] Free society may be an end in itself, or it may be formed for the sake of an ideal. It presupposes natural society but is not essential to the latter. Natural society, on the other hand, arises out of biological necessity. When, as a result of dependence or desire, two or more individuals chance to develop reciprocal interests, society has come into being. Natural society *is,* in this sense, moral and rational, but only secondarily. The family, for instance, being in Santayana's terms a system of mutually adjusted instincts or a community of purpose in which the constituents benefit one another, has acquired moral value or rationality. Significantly, in *Reason in Society,* discussing the "natural" relation of a father to his children, Santayana says he "represents" them, just as he says in *Dominations and Powers* that a ruler should represent his subjects. And as they perpetuate his skills and his outlook, they represent him to posterity. In serving one another's needs parent and child, as organisms equally blind and irrational, become, from the point of view of their respective wills, a rational and a moral unit.

Though Santayana takes society to be a natural growth, his is not an "organismic" theory. Society is composed of organisms but is not an organism itself. Its life is their lives and its moral quality its import for them. While institutions may become autonomous (government, for example), the autonomy is that of the individuals who, having developed vested interests in their institutionalized functions, become "fanatical" in their execution. (Strictly, vested interest must, on the assumption of mechanism, reduce to habitual performance.) True, Santayana endows society with a certain moral importance in that he believes that personal idiosyncrasy and individual talent would, in the state of nature, be trivial and distinction irrelevant. But this value he places on society is not intrinsic or ultimate; it lies in the direction it provides individual endeavor. Among savages, he points out, there are few differences in ability or character. In the demands it makes, a complex society encourages the realization of possibilities which would otherwise remain dormant—or perhaps would not even become possibilities. Environment is therefore a primary factor in the growth of talent and the development of originality. It is, moreover, the *limitations* imposed by a complex and highly specialized society on the primal freedom of the individual which Santayana says stimulate his capacity.[41] The relation between limitation and freedom, which is exemplified here in the relation between individual and society, is the theme of *Dominations and Powers*.

NOTES

[1] *RSoc*, p. 205.

[2] *Ibid.* The concept of moral freedom is an important one for Santayana and will be discussed in detail in connection with *Dominations and Powers*.

[3] Cf. *ibid.*, pp. 32–33.

[4] *RCS*, p. 64.

[5] Cf. "Matter cannot exist without some form, much as by shedding every form in succession it may proclaim its aversion to fixity and its radical formlessness or infinitude. Nor can form, without the treacherous aid of matter, pass from its ideal potentiality into selected and instant being." *RSci*, p. 185. ". . . existence. . . . is the career of a hereditary substance, it is the life of Matter. . . . Matter, as if ashamed at the irrationality of having one form rather than another, hastens to exchange it, whatever it may be, for some other form, and this haste is its whole reality. . . . It is matter, impatient of form, that fills form with a forward tension, and realises one essence after another." *RM*, p. 94.

[6] *RSoc*, p. 70.

[7] *Ibid.*

[8] *Ibid.*, pp. 75–76.

[9] *Ibid.*, p. 44.

[10] *RA*, p. 40.

[11] *RSoc*, p. 78.

[12] *Ibid.*, p. 116.

[13] *Ibid.*, p. 61.

[14] *RCS*, p. 220.

[15] Cf. *RSoc*, pp. 61ff.

[16] *Ibid.*, p. 63.

[17] Cf. *ibid.*, p. 164.

[18] *Ibid.*, p. 137.

[19] *RR*, p. 249.

[20] Cf. *The Realm of Spirit* (New York: Charles Scribner's Sons, 1940), pp. 37–38. Hereafter cited as *RS*. Cf. also *DP*, p. 10.

[21] Cf. *RCS*, p. 26.

[22] *Ibid.*, p. 262.

[23] Cf. "The relevance and truth of science, like the relevance and truth of sense, are pragmatic, in that they mark the actual relations, march, and dis-

tribution of events, in the terms in which they enter our experience." *SE*, p. 257.

[24] *RCS*, p. 166.

[25] *DL*, p. 242.

[26] *RCS*, pp. 166–67.

[27] *RSoc*, p. 191.

[28] Cf. *STT*, pp. 46–47; cf. also p. 10 above, and Chapter V below.

[29] *Ibid.*, p. 140.

[30] *Ibid.*

[31] *Ibid.*, p. 201.

[32] Cf. John W. Bennett and Melvin R. Tumin, *Social Life: Structure and Function* (New York: Alfred A. Knopf, Inc., 1949).

[33] *RSci*, p. 238.

[34] *Ibid.*, p. 102.

[35] *DP*, p. 371.

[36] *RSci*, p. 17.

[37] *RSoc.*, p. 138.

[38] *Ibid.*, p. 189. In *Dominations and Powers* this conception is developed in the notion of a "moral society." Cf. Chapter VIII below.

[39] "The individual belongs to many communities visible and invisible—to communities for which the defining circumstance is publicly articulated and to those for which it is not." Justus Buchler, *Toward a General Theory of Human Judgment* (New York: Columbia University Press, 1951), p. 41.

[40] *RSoc*, p. 189.

[41] Cf. *RSoc*, p. 102.

CHAPTER 5

Biology and Civilization

SOCIETY IS PERPETUALLY EVOLVING, developing both centrifugally and centripetally and becoming increasingly diversified. An individual finds himself enmeshed in innumerable institutional and organizational complexes. His moral involvement in the world increases and his inner life is correspondingly enriched by the introduction of a wealth of symbols expressing the powers and promises of his environment. By virtue of this dual elaboration he is enabled to form gratifying new relationships with others who share in aspects of his life and to live rationally, to understand and appreciate his own nature and the forces that made him what he is. The balance between compulsory affiliation and free adventure, between feeding the body and nourishing the spirit, is what Santayana comes to call, in *Dominations and Powers,* "the economic order of society."[1] In every sphere of social life he is concerned with the economic problem of combining "the maximum of spiritual freedom with the maximum of moral cohesion."[2]

Moral cohesion is the product of shared experience, of a common history. It also, as we shall see, presupposes similar biological endowment. A "moral society," as it is called in *Dominations and Powers,* can be identified, not by territorial boundaries or political relations, but by a tradition which persists in the form of personal character and loyalty to the ancestral sources of that tradition. The ultimate roots of any tradition are in nature at large. "The springs of culture," Santayana characteristically asserts, "go back in the last instance to cosmic forces."[3] The whole history of the universe and of life, the character of the earth, the biologic endowment of the human species are primordial determinants of social life as we encounter it.

The most inclusive community which Santayana considers to be a distinctive force in human history is that which he calls a race. He associates race and civilization but distinguishes between the bearer of civilization and its "fruits."[4] Race emerges from closer analysis as the pattern of traits which determine the character of a society. In this sense a race is not, itself, a society at all. It is as an object of loyalty, of patriotism, that the mythical personification of a race, its "spirit," an ideal which sums up the racial heritage, may be called a society in Santayana's language. This symbolic society is part of the wider ideal society. Viewed as a cultural determinant, however, race is part of nature; it is prior to and conditions the very forms of natural society. Natural society is an existent organization composed of individuals whose heredity is given. Race is a physiological and emotional trait, a set of inheritable qualities which unites individuals by resemblance and affinity as well as by history. Racial characteristics, according to Santayana, are the result of an evolutionary process, and are carried by the "blood," or, to use a more current term, the chromosomes.[5]

Patriotism, loyalty to race or nation (for the most part the terms "race" and "nation" are used interchangeably), relates men in a kind of comradeship, a form of free society in which individuals bind themselves together through common identification with the spirit of their race. Thus, while racial identity is mechanically determined, consciousness of it creates a free society, and it is therefore to be prized. Patriotism is loyalty to one's people or to its genuine representative, a truly benevolent and rational government. When a ruler or regime is venerated but no longer serves or symbolizes the real interests and heritage of the nation, patriotism has degenerated into "idolatry."

In describing patriotism, Santayana aptly characterizes a sentiment which has played an important part in history. Patriotism is as much a matter of policy as of piety. Ethnic factors have, in the long run, been as important as political ones in the generation and resolution of conflict; and the distribution of cultural patterns in the modern world crosses geographic and political boundaries. But Santayana explains these facts by appealing to a concept of race which exhibits not only his personal bias but also some of the weaknesses of an oversimplified materialism. In identifying race with character he confuses the transmission of custom with biologic inheritance and makes national character a function of pedigree.

He conceives race to be associated with social institutions such as language and religion. But "community of race is a far deeper bond than community of language, education, or government."[6] Race is something which underlies these. Again, a race may be identified by its "traditional genius," which is visible in the civilization it has achieved.[7] But civilization is not to be confused with race. It seems one cannot exist without the other, but race, as Santayana defines it, is the ground of culture, not vice versa. Tradition cannot be transplanted to alien soil. "Blood is the ground of character and intelligence," he says. "The fruits of civilization may, indeed, be transmitted from one race to another and consequently a certain artificial homogeneity may be secured amongst different nations; yet unless continual intermarriage takes place each race will soon recast and vitiate the common inheritance."[8]

Poetry, religion, and manners reflect the character of a race but do not shape it. They are in themselves inert and formal, requiring appropriate instincts and habits to keep them alive. On the assumption of epiphenomenalism, these fruits of civilization are largely ideal. They cannot be forces in history but only symptoms of it. Only in so far as it is physically embodied may a cultural product or artifact function causally: "Expression makes thought a power in the very world from which thought drew its being, and renders it in some measure self-sustaining and self-assured."[9] But it is *meaningful* because of factors extrinsic to and existing before it, which have produced it and endowed it with significance. It is a symbol whose whole meaning is "moral," dependent upon the part it is made to play. If the way of life which gave rise to it and in which it plays a significant role has been supplanted by another, such a product has lost its meaning. Thus, steeping ourselves in the literature and art of the Greeks will not make Greeks of us. On the contrary, we will only understand them to the extent that our character and our life still resemble those of the ancients.

Similarly, in the case of contemporary transmission of culture from one people to another the bare fact of assimilation is, as Santayana sees it, a mere surface phenomenon not capable of altering the organisms who are the carriers of culture. If we assume that the character and intelligence of its members determine the style of life in a society and that intelligence and attitudes are tendencies of an organism to respond in particular ways, then these tendencies are the root determinants of culture. If race is somehow associated with "blood," if it is something more than a system of artifacts and set of rules for behavior, it must consist in these "instincts" which are linked to physical, hereditary characteristics. And, if this is the case, then a civilization can be perpetuated only by maintaining the purity of its biological substratum. Conversely, if we desire to combine the characteristics of two cultures, we ought to arrange for hybridization. "Some races," Santayana claims in *Reason in Society,* "are obviously superior to others." This superiority is attributed by him to "a more thorough adjustment to the conditions of existence," to "a painful evolution," and "a prolonged sifting of souls." Thus, he holds, it is rational to object to the fusion of "superior" and "inferior stock," as in the case of white and black peoples.[10] On the other hand, he takes the mixing of what he judges to be "equally gifted" races having complementary cultures to be desirable and even necessary, holding that a "pure" race, as a result of isolation and inbreeding, might have an impoverished culture.

Large contact and concentrated living bring out native genius, but mixture with an inferior stock can only tend to obliterate it. The Jews, the Greeks, the Romans, the English were never so great as when they confronted other nations, reacting against them and at the same time, perhaps adopting their culture; but this greatness fails inwardly whenever contact leads to amalgamation.[11]

The judgment of "superiority" is, on Santayana's own grounds, dogmatic and may be assumed to be representative of the sort of "moralism" which he claims to have later abandoned. More significant theoretically is the biologism which the whole discussion of race reflects.

Santayana acknowledges the fact that traditions are learned and denies that personal character is immutable. Nevertheless, he holds to a distinction between the character of an individual and that of a race, the former being a variation or modification of the latter. And whereas the character of an individual is held to be modified by experience, his racial endowment has been moulded by "breeding and selection."[12] Primary among the factors which shape personal character and determine the direction of individual development are the language, religion, education, and prejudices of his race, factors which he acquires early in life. This acquired bias is his "nationality." Nationality is termed "a natural force and a constituent in character which must be reckoned with." If this is so, since for Santayana all force is physical, nationality must be a physical trait, even though it is distinct from race in being a function of experience rather than heredity. But experience is here taken to be cumulative and effective, and "the historical background of life" to be "a part of its substance."[13] If this is the case, and if race is distinct from nationality, "race" can only mean a hereditary constitutional limit to the educability of a family of individuals. By its unique propensities a race is enabled to develop and pass on, or at least assimilate, a distinctive tradition, or it is prevented from so doing. The genius of a race can be "handed down by inheritance or else by adoption, when the persons adopted can really appreciate the mysteries they are initiated into."[14] A superior culture, then, would be a test of superior racial endowment. But if we do not assume that a race has reached the zenith of its biological or cultural development at a given time, how can such a test be accepted as valid? And what a priori evidence can there be that a given group will or will not assimilate or enrich a culture? If neither empirical nor a priori criteria serve to certify the distinctiveness of races, what assurance have we that race, in the sense of an effective historical force, exists at all?

Furthermore, Santayana does not consistently hold to the distinction between race and nationality. For example he refers to "white and black peoples" as "two nations" and cites the Jews, the Greeks, the Romans, and the English as "races" in some contexts and as "nations" in others. It would seem that his insistence on racial identity is, as he himself suggests, a prejudice, which his materialism enables him to sustain by linking intelligence and character directly, and without empirical justification, to biology. He acknowledges "something unmistakably illiberal, almost superstitious, in standing on race for its own sake, as if origins and not results were of moral value"; he even says that "it matters nothing what blood a man has if he has the right spirit." But he takes "spirit" and "blood" to be linked: "If there is some ground for identifying the two (since monkeys, however educated, are monkeys still) it is only when blood means character and capacity, and is tested by them, that it becomes important."[15]

What Santayana seems to have as his referent in speaking of "character and capacity" or the "genius" of a race is a typical personality which cannot be identified with the language, religion, art, or economic system of a society and which he considers to underlie the latter as causes. The British character, for instance, is portrayed by him as something distinct from English institutions and apparently independent of political or intellectual pretensions. He never seems to consider that it might be a matter of social class. Rather he says that "what governs the Englishman is his inner atmosphere, the weather in his soul." This "is nothing particularly spiritual or mysterious" but "a witness to some settled disposition, some ripening inclination for this or that, deeply rooted in the soul."[16] And for him "soul," or "psyche," is a biological principle distinguished from "spirit," his name for mind or awareness. The former is active, causal, the latter passive.

Other writers have called attention to "national character." Clyde Kluckhohn, for example, writes: "By 'NATIONAL CHARACTER' I mean those modalities of behavior and of view of the world and experience in it that are found or claimed to be characteristic of a specific national or ethnic population at a particular period in time."[17] Erich Fromm calls such a basic personality type the "social character," the nucleus of the character structure which is shared by most members of the same culture in contradistinction to the individual character in which people belonging to the same culture differ from each other."[18] Fromm states that each society impresses this character to some degree upon all the young, moulding them into working parts of the social engine. In order for the social system to function as it does, individuals in various classes and groups must behave in certain ways. The social character moulds and channels their energy so that they *want* to act as they must for the continuance of the society. Anyone required to play a social role will learn to find gratification in socially necessary responses, which fact, rather than hereditary instinct, causes him to follow a social pattern.

On the other hand, Santayana claims that the genius of a race may only be acquired by specially qualified individuals. Rather than being a characteristic of *any* identifiable social entity (as Kluckhohn and Fromm assert), such a genius, he hints, is the property of superior races only: "a general genius

means an exceptional and distinct race."[19] Genius seems to be a variable
dependent upon the evolution of a typical biological character especially
well adapted to its environment. There has evolved, if not a universal human
nature, at least a general character in each great region of the world "on
account of natural conditions which limit forms of life possible in one
region." A poorly adapted or erratically deviant strain would be doomed to
defeat and death. Consequently, "moral integration has occurred very markedly in every good race and society whose members, by adapting themselves
to the same external forces, have created and discovered their common
soul."[20]

On Santayana's hypothesis it would seem that any race or nation which
was not biologically orthodox and therefore morally integrated (i.e., was not
a "good" race) would be doomed to extinction. In fact, not every long-lived
and powerful nation has had a well-integrated culture (for example, the
United States). Conversely, inbred and well-integrated peoples have deterio-
rated politically (for instance, ancient Egypt). Nor has it been proved that
traditional genius is coordinated with anything we could consistently call
race if we take the latter to be something different from the culture pattern
itself. Groups that are closely related biologically have evolved divergent
cultures, and unrelated peoples often show striking similarities. These phenomena are seemingly explicable only in historical and environmental
terms. Ruth Benedict stresses this in connection with similarities and differences among American Indian cultures which cross the lines of biological
relatedness. She points out, in addition, that if we consider the distribution of
culture patterns in time, rather than in geography, it is even more apparent
that variations of culture and behavior do not depend on biological variations. In the history of Western civilization this is especially well illustrated.
Benedict calls attention, for example, to the fact that in the Middle Ages
Europeans were as prone to mystic behavior, to epidemics of psychic phenomena, as they were in the nineteenth century to the most hard-headed
materialism. The culture changed a fundamental bias without any corre-
sponding change in the racial constitution of the people.[21]

Santayana, however, draws a distinction between "fashions" in behavior
and thought and something more permanent. He recognizes that education
and contagion may be powerful influences on behavior and therefore
acknowledges that "it may seem a prejudice to insist on race, turning its
assumed efficacy into a sheer dogma, with fanatical impulses behind it"; yet
he insists that education and environment are insufficient to sustain a given
model of behavior for long and that, therefore, they cannot account for that
persistence of a fashion which turns it into a tradition. And "nothing," he
says, "is more treacherous than tradition when insight and force are lacking

to keep it warm."[22] "Insight" and "force" apparently refer to the racial tendencies which shape and perpetuate tradition. But it is hard to see how these differ, except in duration, from the forces that sustain fashions or make for social change. To support his position, Santayana would have had to demonstrate independently the existence of generic and persistent "racial" impulses which outweigh those that may prevail at a given time.

The notion of race would be demonstrably superfluous if it could be shown that national character is itself an institution, originating in and perpetuated by events occurring at the level of natural society. George Herbert Mead, in fact, identifies social institutions with what Fromm calls social character, explaining the genesis and persistence of the latter, not in terms of passive inheritance, but of active role-taking.[23] Mead shows how self and mind are essentially social, only arising in the social process. He defines social institutions as organized sets of responses to given situations, forms of group activity which are learned by the members of a community. These "generalized social attitudes" enter into the very nature of the individual, his self, so that in any situation he can "take the attitude" of the others involved and behave appropriately toward them. Thus, wherever there is a society, there is a social character which is both social and personal and is learned, rather than biologically engendered.

Santayana, on the contrary, views the self as a biological phenomenon (which in his later works he calls "the psyche") and considers the mind to be a product of bodily life, a light kindled occasionally by the "automatic inward machinery that executes the marvellous work."[24] In his system mind and self are both essentially individual, though they may be involved in social interaction and alter to some extent in response to external stimuli. "One of the great lessons," therefore, "which society has to teach its members is that society exists. The child, like the animal, is a colossal egotist, not from a want of sensibility, but through his deep transcendental isolation. The mind is naturally its own world and its solipsism needs to be broken down by social influence."[25] Thought may be elicited by stimuli; it may occasionally be "practical"—appropriate to its circumstances, be these personal or social; but whatever its secondary properties, it is intrinsically lonely and passive reception, "a private echo and response" to the body's ambient motions.[26]

It would be difficult to build a conception of social character on the basis of such an individualist definition of the self and the mind. Santayana tries to account for sociality by means of the concept of unanimity, postulating a shared (i.e., racial) organic or physical structure onto which similar experience grafts similar character and similar understanding. To the extent that persons having the same "organization" undergo similar experiences, he suggests, they will have the same logic and the same moral standards.

"Unanimity in thought involves identity of functions and similarity of organs. These conditions mark off the sphere of rational communication and society; where they fail altogether there is no mutual intelligence, no conversation, no moral solidarity."[27] On his view, two selves or psyches can be similar only if they have a similar heredity. (In *Dominations and Powers,* where this theory is reaffirmed, historical repetition is linked to the propagation of kinds of organisms through "seeds" which are "almost exactly similar.")[28] Two minds can be alike only by reflecting similar histories. Similar organisms passing through analogous experiences will have minds which will resemble and can therefore understand one another. Thus, they will constitute a society, but these spirits will themselves have no vital relationship. Social relatedness, for Santayana, consists in physical dependence and/or shared interests, but the essence of sharing in most cases seems to be paralleling. "True society," he says, "is limited to similar beings leading similar lives and enabled by the contagion of their common habits and arts to attribute to one another, each out of his own experience, what the other actually endures."[29] This concept of society is elaborated in *Dominations and Powers* in the notion of a "moral society."

Mead, separating the self from the organism, holds that the former is wholly a social structure. He considers the self to be absent at birth and to develop only in the course of social interaction and communication. "Moral solidarity" and "mutual intelligence," on this view, presuppose not just structural similarity but interaction *within a social system* as well. Communication is established by participation in this system; it is not necessary for individuals "to attribute to one another, each out of his own experience, what the other actually endures," for, as Mead sees it, social "experience" is commonly available.

Both Santayana and Mead give symbols a central role in the social process, but, according to Santayana, their function is derivative, dependent upon the existence of minds able to understand them. He comes closest to Mead in his appreciation of the role of language but fails, I think, to develop its implications. Mead values language as a vehicle of participation and communication which, embodying the institutional structure of society, both enables an individual to relate to others and contributes to the development of his mind. Society, he insists, does not simply stamp a pattern on the behavior of an individual: it actually gives him a mind. Mind, for Mead, is not sheer consciousness, but the structure whereby one reflects on experience and communicates with oneself (literally "consciously conversing" with oneself) in terms of the social attitudes which one has internalized. The structure of the mind, like that of language, reflects the pattern of the society's organized behavior, imposing general outlines on the conduct of the individual. Still more important, as well as mediating the impact of the society on the individual in such a way as to allow for variation, the mind "enables him in turn to stamp the pattern of his further developing self (further developing through his mental activity) upon the structure or organization of human society, and thus in a degree to reconstruct and modify in terms of his self the general pattern of social or group behavior in terms of which his self was originally constituted."[30]

According to Santayana, thought, rather than being a means of reconstructing either the self or society, is "an experience realised, not a force to be used."[31] Language, rather than being integral to the self and the social order, is "an artificial means of establishing unanimity and transferring thought from one mind to another."[32] Mutual understanding, for Santayana, just as for Mead, depends upon taking the attitude of the other: "Every symbol or phrase, like every gesture, throws the observer into an attitude to which a certain idea corresponded in the speaker; to fall exactly into the speaker's attitude is exactly to understand."[33] But Santayana believes this communication to unite atomic individuals, whereas Mead takes mutuality to constitute the self. Like Santayana, Mead relates the meanings of things to organic factors in the individual, specifically, the structure of the central nervous system. But he can only understand the latter as a mediating element operating within a social context. Intelligent behavior is "essentially and fundamentally social." The life process which it presupposes is an ongoing *social* process. The unity of this process—"or of any one of its component acts—is irreducible, and in particular cannot be adequately analyzed simply into a number of discrete nerve elements."[34] The organization of an individual's behavior, then, is provided by the social process in which he is involved. Whatever functions are performed by the central nervous system are solicited by and have reverberations for that process. "Individual" acts are *primarily* social, even though they are perforce biological, and Mead rejects any analysis that isolates neurological factors, for such isolation renders them meaningless as far as conduct is concerned.

Santayana is more interested in showing how the social order rests on material foundations and consequently emphasizes the part played by the biological individual in the social process and, in particular, in linguistic activity. "Language is accordingly an overflow of the physical basis of thought. It is an audible gesture, more refined than the visible, but in the same sense an automatic extension of nervous and muscular processes."[35] The use of the expression "an audible gesture" is striking in its resemblance to Mead's conception of the gesture as the model of communicative activity. But Mead denies the automatism Santayana attributes to gestures and holds their occurrence to be explicable only in the context of social interaction. In addition, for Santayana, these processes must become socialized ex post facto; in comparison with Mead's presentation, his view seems forced and wanting: "Spontaneous expression, if it is to be recognisable and therefore in effect expressive, labours under the necessity of subordinating itself to an ideal system of expressions, a permanent language in which its spontaneous utterances may be embedded. By virtue of such adoption into a common medium expression becomes interpretable. . . ."[36]

Since he holds that "to be actual and self-existent is to be individual," Santayana may be understood as taking individuals to be ontologically prior to society.[37] The natural society of a man and a woman is requisite for the birth of an individual, but this circumstance is not shown to be incompatible with the atomistic conception of a society composed of individuals who may, nevertheless, exist as individuals in the absence of that society. Mead, on the contrary, would say that there can be no individuals as such apart from society. It is sometimes contended that only individuals exist, and therefore, societies per se are not existents. Yet at times Santayana suggests the existence of social entities: "corporate bodies" are said to be the temporal existents to which the term "natural society" calls attention; material "organisms," which may be individual or social, are asserted to underlie and occasion mental and moral life.[38] Society, thus existent, can be influential. Were Santayana content to credit "the political and historical forces" which "determine . . . familiar institutions," he might have dispensed with race in favor of nationality.[39] But his materialism makes a biological, as opposed to a sociological, interpretation of group identity plausible; and his atomism and epiphenomenalism make a sociological explanation inadequate since society for him is a secondary order.

We cannot deny that Santayana believes human nature to be greatly influenced by the social process in which it is involved. He seems to think, like Mead, that "society" is essential to the understanding of "humanity," the latter being a product of "that region of common experience, traditional feeling, and conventional thought which all minds enter at birth and can elude only at the risk of inward collapse and extinction."[40] Also like Mead, he claims that human nature at any time and in any place is a product of natural evolution. The question is to what degree he understands that evolution and that structure to be biological and to what extent he takes them to be social, a matter of changing conventions not involving any modification of instinct or capacity. His reluctance to abandon the biological concept of race is obvious: in Dominations and Powers he continues to say that "war will be disastrous from a humanistic point of view if the new race is of inferior blood, or if with the race that has succumbed the aptitude for a high organisation has disappeared."[41] Race is said there to be not just "a real difference in the soul" but a desirable expression of liberty and a vehicle of cultural advance; it is also said "that the secret of moral progress is inbreeding, which allows the special potentialities in one incipient variety of human beings to develop." This line of thought is integrated with the pluralistic political ideal established in *Dominations and Powers,* so that "the cultivation of *different* characters and arts, when such characters or arts are opportune, is therefore requisite for the emergence of any eminent beauty, culture, genius, or virtue."[42]

A metaphysics which places all efficacy in matter is compatible with the notion that there are racial traits which are physical and are causal influences in history. That Santayana does not consider them the only causal factors is amply demonstrated, but he attaches overwhelming importance to them. But naturalism is also coherent with the view that the organization of individuals in a system has consequences both for the members of that system and for the more inclusive orders in which it is implicated. Such a structure is a power in the world and an agent in its own future development. That Santayana recognizes this is illustrated in his discussion of the family as a social institution. Once established, he points out, the family takes on innumerable secondary functions, becoming a very different social organ from that which it started out to be. As part of natural society it is efficacious as a point of departure for other institutions, economic, educational, and so forth. In fact, he says in *Reason in Society,* "all society at present rests on this institution, so that we cannot easily discern which of our habits and sentiments are parcels of it, and which are attached to it adventitiously and have an independent basis."[43] It is noteworthy that, despite the role he assigns to instinct in maintaining tradition, Santayana believes the family as an institution—and every other institution grown political—to have outrun the instincts which it serves: "In no civilised community, for instance, has the union of man and wife been limited to its barely necessary period. It has continued after the family was reared and has remained life-long; it has commonly involved a common dwelling and religion and often common friends and property."[44]

In insisting upon the fact of race, Santayana is suggesting that there is a limit beyond which social institutions cannot penetrate individual character. This limit is provided in part by biological traits which are common to the members of a race. Had Santayana elaborated the conception of political society, he might, perhaps, have evolved a political theory of race which was no less naturalistic yet was more adequate than the biological one he offers us.

NOTES

[1] *DP,* p. 25.
[2] *RSoc,* p. 58.
[3] *Ibid.,* p. 164.
[4] *Ibid.,* p. 165.
[5] *Ibid.*
[6] *Ibid.*
[7] *Ibid.,* p. 169.
[8] *Ibid.,* p. 165.
[9] *RSci,* p. 180.
[10] *RSoc,* pp. 166–67.
[11] *Ibid.,* p. 167.
[12] *Ibid.,* p. 173.
[13] *Ibid.,* p. 174. Note that "experience" according to this usage would have to be a process underlying consciousness rather than "conscious experience."
[14] *Ibid.,* p. 169.
[15] *Ibid.,* p. 167.   .
[16] *SE,* p. 30.
[17] *Culture and Behavior* (Glencoe, Illinois: The Free Press, 1962), p. 210.
[18] *The Sane Society* (New York: Holt, Rinehart and Winston, 1955), p. 78.
[19] *RSoc,* p. 168.
[20] *RCS,* pp. 281–82.
[21] *Patterns of Culture* (New York: Houghton Mifflin, 1934).
[22] *RSoc,* p. 168.
[23] *Mind, Self and Society* (Chicago: University of Chicago Press, 1934).
[24] *RCS,* p. 214.
[25] *RSoc,* p. 48.
[26] *RCS,* p. 207.
[27] *Ibid.,* p. 278.
[28] *DP,* p. 219.
[29] *RCS,* p. 159.
[30] Mead, *op. cit.,* p. 263.
[31] *RCS,* p. 214.
[32] *Ibid.,* pp. 153–54.
[33] *Ibid.,* p. 154.
[34] Mead, *op. cit.,* p. 118.
[35] *RSci,* p. 181.
[36] *Ibid.,* p. 184.
[37] *RCS,* p. 279.
[38] *RSoc,* p. 137.

[39] *Ibid.*, pp. 161–62.
[40] *RCS*, p. 274.
[41] *DP*, p. 218.
[42] *Ibid.*, p. 358.
[43] *RSoc*, p. 47.
[44] *Ibid.*, p. 43.

CHAPTER 6

Moral Idealism and Moral Rationality

THE CONTRAST between Santayana's earlier and later works has been a major concern of commentators. He acknowledged a shift in his point of view but denied any modification of his naturalism. When *The Life of Reason* was reissued in 1922, he proclaimed the change in his thought to be one of interest or focus, not entailing any major alteration in his system:

> After all, there has been no change in my deliberate doctrine; only some changes of mental habit. I now dwell by preference on other perspectives, in which the same objects appear with their relative bulks reversed, and inversely hiding one another; what lay before in the background—nature—has come forward, and the life of reason, which then held the centre of the stage, has receded.[1]

The claim that the so-called reversal was not a systematic change is indeed tenable, and developments in his moral and political philosophy seem to confirm that it was, at least in part, a change of focus, a shift in what a Gestalt psychologist would call the figure-ground relation. Whereas *The Life of Reason* is a critical study of intellectual and cultural phenomena whose fate it is to be engendered and extinguished, *Realms of Being* is an imaginative construction of the reality which its author thinks we must necessarily posit to account for our conscious life in the first place. The articulation of his ontology seems to have led Santayana to an enhanced recognition of the dependence of mind upon the vicissitudes of the irrational flux of matter. This recognition is paralleled by several modifications of his philosophy of society: he adopted a new definition of rational order; he ceased to consider a universal, stable, and widely satisfying civilization to be possible; and there was a change in his moral (or "political" in the broad sense) position, a revision of his earlier normative stance. That is to say, he was led to a growing acceptance of diverse modes in art and life, to an increasing catholicity of taste, and eventually to the pluralistic ideal of *Dominations and Powers*.

It can be shown, I believe, that most of the categories of *Realms of Being* are present in *The Life of Reason,* although they are not written with initial capital letters. More to the point, matter, essence, truth, and spirit stand in the same mutual relations in Santayana's earliest writings as those to which his later metaphysics assigns them. From the first, Santayana believed all causation to be material and mechanical and relegated thought to the status of an epiphenomenon, a helpless reflection of events which transpire at the physical level. The import of his doctrine, however, is not consistently acknowledged in *The Life of Reason,* where, despite the recognition of the implication of epiphenomenalism that "the Life of Reason is not a power but a result," it is considered natural and possible for reason "to adjust all demands to one ideal and adjust that ideal to its natural conditions."[2] This tendency to moral idealism in its most lofty and poetic form is there termed "spirituality" and, together with "piety" and "charity," marks that form of the life of reason which is portrayed in *Reason in Religion.*

By the twenties Santayana saw certain pessimistic implications of his view of matter as all-powerful and essentially irrational. He came to view the life of reason, he said, as "a decidedly episodical thing, polyglot, interrupted, insecure." Therefore, he asserted, he could not take the different phases of art, religion, or philosophy as seriously as he had and found himself "less eager to choose and to judge among them, as if only one form could be right."[3] This disillusioned viewpoint characterizes all of Santayana's "later" works, including *Dominations and Powers.* It entails a revised conception of the significance and function of *ideals* which marks the greatest departure of that work from the position taken in *The Life of Reason.* The magnification of the forces underlying the formulation and pursuit of ideals resulted in a reappraisal of moral idealism and a modification of the "Socratic" method of rational ethics.

In his critical study of the changing roles of ideals and essences in Santayana's philosophy (referred to in Chapter III) Munitz discusses some of the ramifications of this change in moral philosophy, calling attention to the "mystical abandonment of moral idealism" that marks what Munitz interprets as a shift from a rational to a post-rational morality.[4] Munitz holds that this shift involved elevating the spiritual life to the position originally held by the life of reason. And whereas the life of reason was identified with moral idealism, Munitz contends that spirituality (which Santayana progressively redefined) finally evolved into perfectly detached and intellectual contemplation, the direct antithesis of a moral or political interest in existence. Spirituality is portrayed, in *Platonism and the Spiritual Life* and in *The Realm of Spirit,* predominantly (although, as Munitz indicates, not with perfect consistency) as the disinterested contemplation of essences.

When viewed by pure spirit "under the form of eternity," the forms which immediate experience presents to us are taken in these books to constitute pure Being as distinct from existence. This is the thesis of "mysticism"; for a mystic, the highest achievement of spirit is to withdraw from morality altogether. In *Reason in Religion* the mystic's withdrawal had been condemned as irrational.[5]

It seems to me that in Santayana's political writings the alteration in his moral philosophy takes a form somewhat different from that described by Munitz. The change is linked to a revision in the concept of moral rationality. Santayana ceased to identify moral idealism and spirituality with the life of reason, seeing them now as natural and valuable developments in the lives of conscious, moral beings but as no longer central to rationality. Santayana himself claimed that he had always seen rationality and spirituality as two dimensions of human life rather than successive and mutually exclusive stages. He writes in a letter to Justus Buchler:

. . . what people . . . dislike is not so much the materialism or ontology slipped under the life of reason, as the "spiritual life" supposed to be substituted for it in my estimation.

That is a complete misconception . . . the rationality of . . . life and its spirituality might be called two concomitant dimensions of it, the one lateral and the other vertical. The vertical or spiritual dimension is what inward religion has always added to life in the world.[6]

In "A General Confession" he states that "between the spiritual life and the life of reason there is accordingly no contradiction: they are concomitant: yet there is a difference of temper and level, as there is between agriculture and music."[7] The difference seems to be that agriculture is purposive, music disinterested: reason pursues ends, spirit realizes forms, ideas, and dialectical relations.

In *The Life of Reason* existence is examined primarily as the background of intelligent life, and civilization is viewed, at least ideally, as a progressive harmonization of natural tendencies in the light of equally natural and widely shared (and recognized) needs and interests. Thus, nature is seen to give rise to the life of reason. Human life can be not just occasionally rational but is characteristically and increasingly so. And rational adjustment, the method of intelligence, is optimistically held to dominate its mechanical and physical conditions. Nature fosters not merely awareness but the successful pursuit of ideals. "The life of reason" is the name "for that part of experience which perceives and pursues ideals—all conduct so controlled and all sense so interpreted as to perfect natural happiness."[8] Ideals consciously entertained, visions aesthetic, practical, religious, moral, scientific, or political are taken to be the medium in which man's adjustment to his world is not simply reflected but effectively reflected upon. Human life can be an art and moral idealism is natural wisdom and the culmination of the rational life. In *The Life of Reason* Santayana takes the formulation of ideals to be generic and what he there terms spirituality, i.e., "life in the ideal," to be "the fundamental and native type of all life."[9] The life of reason is that life in which, as a result of training and experience, of the "docility" and "plasticity" of the organism, a man can develop purposes which will be achieved. Where these are conscious, thought can be "practical."

Life, he says in *Reason in Religion,* can be rational at all levels, even the primitive and sensual. At the level of primary impulses and elementary values, rationality consists in simple pleasures and spontaneous adjustment. At the level of instrumental processes and discursive thought, art and science introduce rationality into an otherwise incoherent existence, and love and friendship are the rational satisfactions of the heart. But rationality in these areas is only occasionally achieved, and it is only by formulating a comprehensive ideal that reason is made to encompass the whole of life. "Spirituality," in this context, is the conception of a highest, or ultimate, good which unifies and gives meaning to the seemingly vain and often contradictory pursuits to which we are by nature committed. Spirituality transcends partial rationality by providing a purpose for life itself, turning it from a blind into a knowing enterprise with a promise of success. Santayana here seems to be portraying spirituality as ultimate rationality, the perfection of moral idealism, which confers a moral order on the natural chaos in which we find ourselves. The life of reason, for a being capable of it, can only be a life in which ultimate ideals play a part; conversely, "a spiritual human life . . . would have to be rational and to form some representation of man's total environment and interests."[10]

It is only later in Santayana's career that spiritual life came to be clearly defined as the life of *pure* spirit, emancipated from impulse. In *Platonism and the Spiritual Life* the role of spirit in the moral life is described as the sheer *realization* of values which, as realized, felt or conceived, are in themselves essences. In Santayana's late political philosophy, however, spirituality in this sense plays only an indirect part. By asserting the equal legitimacy of all ideals he may be said, in *Dominations and Powers,* to approach more nearly a "spiritual" viewpoint than that of natural morality. But the book is openly and conspicuously moral in tone, despite the relative disillusion in its moral stance.

As a young man, Santayana took the civilization of ancient Greece to be of all civilizations the most nearly rational because it was an exemplar of moral idealism. Socrates, Plato, and Aristotle worked at developing a satisfactory model of the moral life. They thought the rational thing to do was to strive to know the whole truth about themselves, and in learning it they believed they would know the secret of their own happiness. Like the Christians, they were wrong in believing that their own view of the world was or could ever be unbiased and completely adequate. But unlike modern man, the Greeks were not lost in the universe. In believing "that there was a single solid natural wisdom to be found, that reason could find it, and that mankind, sobered by reason, could put it in practice," they had found the secret of freedom.[11] Even in *The Life of Reason* the limitation on the possibility of rationality in everyday existence is recognized. But the truly rational, spiritual man described in *Reason in Religion* is said to know "how to interpret the casual rationalities in the world and isolate their principle, setting this principle up in the face of nature as nature's standard and model."[12]

In *Dominations and Powers* to set up a standard or model for nature would be judged egotistical. Santayana seems now to have been more aware of and more nearly resigned to the immense complexity and confusion of nature and to have accepted the view that since man is tied to this universe for his well-being, he is destined to learn the futility of moral idealism. Although we can escape the cares of this world in the contemplation of ideals, and to do so is a kind of freedom, ultimate aims have lost their former place in the moral life. And, in fact, the fragmentation and complexity of both private and public life precludes their development. "What a man lives for is hardly better known to a man, or less often falsely described in orations, than what a government works for. There are, for both, incidental successes and failures clearly distinguishable, but ultimate aims are not discerned, for the excellent reason that they do not exist."[13] Moral idealism, while it is healthy and a sign of strength because it represents the integrity of a psyche or self, is not rational when it reaches too far and defies the limitations imposed by its environment; for psyche thereby loses its freedom. Moral rationality now consists in "rational cooperation with circumstances." There are two stages in this cooperation: one involves modifying the means we employ in order to reach our chosen goal; the other is "a deeper stage when we suspend a given aim, substituting another no less truly compatible with our primal will and vital liberty" but, perhaps, less ambitious and, at least, more likely to be attained. That is, it is rational to abandon moral idealism when we find an ideal hopelessly remote; politics, "being a moral art, sets human, not cosmic, standards."[14]

Rational ethics, in *Reason in Science,* is a matter of acquiring self-knowledge and coordinating interests. Rational government, in *Dominations and Powers* (for Santayana, as for Plato and Aristotle, the principles of government are the same for the individual and for society), depends more heavily upon the recognition of circumstances, in addition to knowledge of psyche, that is, the needs of the organism. Moral rationality in each case implies discipline, but the primary emphasis in the earlier work is optimistically placed on the mutual adjustment of interests. "To rationalize an interest is simply to correlate it with every other interest which it at all affects."[15] In *Reason in Science* rational ethics is contrasted with the Stoic ideal of rationality. Instead of focussing on the harmonization of motives, the Stoics emphasized disillusioned conformity to nature. This motif is not wholly absent from *The Life of Reason,* but *Dominations and Powers,* with its stress on obedience to the authority of "things" or of "circumstances," is closer to the Stoic teaching. Moral rationality in the later book is actually an amalgamation of Stoic and Socratic rationality, but the Stoic aspect becomes more pronounced.

Viewed in the setting of his political philosophy, Santayana's change of interest does not appear to have been a *metanoia* but an increased emphasis on natural causes and limitations, as he claimed, a strengthening, not a weakening, of "naturalism." This results in greater appreciation of the power of circumstances and leads to reservations about the importance of harmonizing ideals, a devaluation of moral idealism. It also engenders an increased emphasis on the diversity and variation, rather than the constancy, in human nature, with the corollary that Santayana holds that the rational ideal would be to foster diversity as far as possible, rather than emphasize the harmonization of interests.[16] The focus on nature and mechanism also results in enhanced respect on his part for habit, custom, and tradition, with the consequence that his conservatism is reinforced.

The *Life of Reason* is itself an exercise in moral idealism, an exploration of the possibility of a rational civilization, which would, by its very nature, be universally acceptable. The ideal of society presented here is a perfectly stable state, unified, as is an ideal family, and harmoniously serving the interests of all. In *Reason in Society* Santayana formulates such an ideal in the form of a natural aristocracy in which those who rule are representative, not just as parents are, but also in the sense of being eminent or excellent, approaching perfection in the type of citizen. But in other contexts his idealism is qualified by the conception of nature (which of course includes human nature) as fundamentally and irrationally diverse. "A rational life touches the irrational at its core as well as at its periphery. In both directions it meets physical force and can subsist only by exercising physical force in return. The range of rational ethics is limited to the intermediate political zone, in which existences have attained some degree of natural unanimity."[17] This zone is narrow. Nevertheless, the concept of a perfectly rational social order is held to be legitimate and its formulation to be part of rational politics. But in *Dominations and Powers* Santayana denies the legitimacy of a universal political ideal because he denies the possibility of the harmony of powers which would be required to support it. Nature imposes "a double veto" on political idealism. First, the complexity of human nature and society makes it absolutely impossible ever to serve all interests in the same system. And second, if this were momentarily possible, a stable society could not survive in a world that is perpetually changing.[18] There can, then, be no fixed ideal of society. But the concept of a "rational order of society" which is introduced in *Dominations and Powers* is a different kind of ideal, based on a definition of moral rationality which does not subordinate living ideals to merely imagined ones, or to more inclusive ones such as the ideal of harmony.

Compared with the earlier text, the preface to the second edition of *The Life of Reason* assigns a no less important but more tenuous place to thought and to ideals. Methodologically, the stream of consciousness is always central in Santayana's system. "The immediate flux" is always his starting point, as he states it to be in the original introduction to *The Life of Reason:* "Here, then, is the programme of the following work: Starting with the immediate flux, in which all objects and impulses are given, to describe the Life of Reason. . . ."[19] It must be remembered that for Santayana "objects" are ideal terms which may stand for other things but are per se conscious ideas and, as such, are intrinsically different from the forces which they may symbolize. In *The Life of Reason,* it will be recalled, the given is said to exist; in *Realms of Being* the distinction between what is given and material existence is sharpened: "That which is certain and given" is the data of intuition, "something of which existence cannot be predicated."[20] In both places, that which is present in consciousness is the actuality from which the material world is merely inferred. In all his writings Santayana takes consciousness to be not merely the starting point of speculation but also the supreme achievement of physical nature. Paradoxically, the most significant thing he can assert concerning consciousness, especially in his later works, is its radical dependence upon material, irrational, premoral existence, the actuality of which he can only postulate.

In a universe governed by matter, whose tendencies thought merely reflects, thought cannot literally dominate, or even know, existence, as Santayana repeatedly says. Acceptance of this doctrine results in a certain humility with regard to the products of thought and of art, which is apparent even in *The Life of Reason.* In *Reason in Common Sense* spirit is ironically and even despairingly portrayed as speaking to itself about things it does not understand for reasons it cannot fathom. The "products" of the human imagination really emanate from a "deeper" biological self which cannot be known or controlled and, in this sense, Santayana ironically asserts, cannot even be said to be our own. The visions of spirit belong to ideal society; there is no certainty that they are ever representative of anything beyond themselves. They may be interesting or beautiful and make the private world richer, and their presence may be reassuring, but these ideal objects are neither intrinsically rational nor of instrumental value. "The oracles of spirit all have to be discounted. They are uttered in a cave."[21]

For Santayana, to say that art is the flower of life and not an instrument is not to denigrate it. But he takes art, religion, common sense, and science to be similarly epiphenomenal, and they turn out, on his assumptions, to be similarly poetic. I feel that the poetic dimension of common sense, science, and philosophy is usually underrated by laymen and philosophers alike. Santayana justly emphasizes it, but in so doing he has difficulty accounting for the practical efficacy of reason and the power of science. He cautions that we must not think that religion (which he likens to poetry) is science, but he sometimes seems to reduce science to poetry and to confuse it with myth.

As a materialist, Santayana would assess the various forms of religion, science, and art solely in relation to the natural interests from which they emanate. And since these, in the cosmos he posits, are various and conflicting, the cultural phenomena to which they give rise are, in their existence and worth, incommensurable. This judgment is stated by Democritus in Santayana's Dialogue, "Normal Madness": "What madness to assert that one collocation of atoms or one conjunction of feelings is right or is better, and another is wrong or is worse!"[22] This is the position toward which Santayana himself was moving. In the preface to *Dominations and Powers* he claims that the kind of moralism of *The Life of Reason*, where he had evaluated and compared human institutions, trying to decide which were better and more rational, has now to be abandoned. "I have become aware," he adds, "that anyone's sense of what is good and beautiful must have a somewhat narrow foundation, namely his circumstances and his particular brand of human nature."[23] Nevertheless, Santayana's acceptance of "this limitation in all moral dogmatism" appears to be not anything new, but a necessary consequence of the naturalist view of morality developed in *Reason in Science*. There morality is clearly defined as a function of interest or intent, and the dogmatic character of all moral judgments, however reasoned or justified, is explicitly recognized and accepted as essential to any criticism, since criticism is, of necessity, the enterprise of a specific being with needs and a direction of its own. But the dogmatic position of reason need not be uncritically dogmatic; "on the contrary, it is the sophistical position that is uncritically neutral. All criticism needs a dogmatic background, else it would lack objects and criteria for criticism."[24]

Santayana does not appear to have altered his conception of the nature and foundations of morality and ethics but to have changed his own moral position. Not, as he sometimes claimed, that he eschewed ideals altogether: he remained a moralist and a critic. But the goal he desired for men altered in conformity with his intensified version of materialism. The "shift" in his critical stance was, not to mysticism, but toward what he called a "cosmic" view. That is, he saw that in *The Life of Reason* he had attempted to view cultural history in the light of his own preferences but without acknowledging his bias. Subsequently, he tried to adopt a perspective more appropriate to a naturalistic cosmology, one in which no "moral center" was to take precedence over any other (other cosmologies admittedly being possible). That is, he attempted to assimilate his position as closely as possible— and Santayana was always explicitly aware of the limited extent to which this could be achieved—to that of an ideal, disinterested scientist, a "free spirit." (In its lack of partisanship, science is said, in *Platonism and the Spiritual Life,* to resemble spirituality.) In a letter to John Yolton, replying to the latter's criticism of his moralizing in *Dominations and Powers,* Santayana writes that he feels Yolton's real objection is, not to the fact of moralizing, but to the moral position taken. He points out that naturalism has its own way of accounting for moral judgments—the materialist hypothesis—which places morality in a secondary position in nature. Description, the scientific part of political philosophy, therefore "envelops" preference, the philosophic part, as nature envelops morals. "But," he writes, "the prenatal history of morals, or all natural history, does not belittle *morally* any of its data."[25] In other words, as a scientist investigating morals, Santayana still considers himself a materialist. As a moral philosopher, he now professes to judge moral phenomena in the light of naturalism and from the point of view of the cosmos as a whole rather than that of any of its parts. He has come to look upon this sort of moral transcendence as natural to man and a distinguishing characteristic of intellect. Intellect first arises in the struggle for survival, but it is essential to it that it "disengages itself from that servile office (which is that of its organ only) and from the beginning is speculative and impartial in its own outlook, and thinks it not robbery to take the point of view of God, of the truth, and of eternity."[26] To (his) intellect, any man is just one among all others. Morality, therefore, as it becomes increasingly intelligent, can approach science in disinterestedness. This is the position from which, in *Dominations and Powers,* Santayana claims he tries to view the world, its history, and its political life.

Santayana conceives moral judgment to be the expression of individual perspective, the result of the interaction of organism and environment. Impulsive and conscious individuals, in reflecting upon the situations in which they find themselves, judge things to be favorable or unfavorable, introducing moral considerations into the world. A judgment that something is good is a statement based upon awareness of all the relevant factors. Values in this way emerge in consciousness and may properly be said to be present only to awareness. Thus, only spirit incarnate can *realize* values; it is only in consciousness that they are *actual*. As a consequence, in *Reason in Society* Santayana adopts the position that the moral worth of a social organization is its import in the conscious lives of its members, i.e., the position of individualism. At the same time he holds that the reflective moralist, if he recognizes the diversity and incompatibility of natural interests and of spontaneous or intuitive moral judgments, will have as a goal the harmonization of those interests. Santayana believes this ideal of harmony to be grounded in real individual interest and to be at least partially attainable. While he claims that conflict has a biological basis, he also claims, in *The Life of Reason,* that human beings possess an impulse to synthesize and harmonize experience. This impulse, which, he says, introduces method into moral judgment, he calls *reason*—one of several senses he gives to that word. And the direct aim of reason is said to be *harmony*. Whereas the source of all value and all morality is the particular needs of individuals, reason transcends these needs, positing a more inclusive end or ideal. And whereas each ideal, by virtue of its natural status, is its own justification, reason leads us toward even more comprehensive ideals, so that we can conceive an ultimate social ideal, based on the totality of human needs, which becomes "a test of general progress."[27]

The Life of Reason, treating of civilization, finds in the culture of the Greeks a standard of moral idealism and moral rationality. The Greek ideals—piety, country, friendship, and beauty—were all humanly relevant and realizable. The relations of the Greek gods to men were no mystery; they lived among men and intervened in human affairs. Their influence was present and intelligible, but they did not dictate to men what their ends, or the means by which they were to attain them, ought to be—these were held to be a function of human nature. It is in ethics that Santayana finds the Greeks most admirable. Every society must develop its own culture and morality, but, says Santayana, "we can adopt from Greek morals . . . the abstract principle of their development; their foundation in all the extant forces of human nature and their effort toward establishing a perfect harmony among them."[28]

In *Dominations and Powers* harmony is no longer the prime goal. As I have suggested, it is the diversity within human nature which is stressed rather than its uniformity, its variability rather than its stability. In society, as in nature at large, the multiplicity of forms attained by the flux of matter proliferates incompatible ends which cannot be reconciled, even though to pure spirit they may seem logically compatible. In deference to the divergence in nature, the progressive unification of interests is altogether renounced in favor of "the principle of spiritual wealth in spiritual liberty," or what Santayana calls "moral freedom." That is, he now stresses the cultivation of the natural diversity of established societies to encompass and preserve the radical diversity among men.

On the grounds that a rational interest is an interest in harmony and that reason dictates an enlarged sympathy, Santayana had claimed, in *Reason in Society*, that rationality in a particular government insured universal applicability and that universal rationality could be attained by the leaders of a given society. Thus, an ideal government, despite its historical uniqueness, would be a vehicle through which reason could rule the world, and "a dream of universal predominance visiting a truly virtuous people could be an aspiration toward universal beneficence."[29] Even if good government were imposed forcibly on others, it would be beneficial, for a ruler is good to the extent that he identifies with, fosters, and harmonizes those interests which are most deeply human and widely shared. In this sense, any government may be "representative," not just of its people, but of any and every nation, "for every man who is governed at all must be governed by others."[30]

In *Dominations and Powers*, however, where he is more concerned with world government, Santayana insists that local and national bias is part of the essence of a government and, moreover, that it is both difficult to eradicate and precious. Only the most fundamental biological characteristics are universal; therefore, a "universal" government would have to be one with no culture whatsoever. It "must have no arbitrary moral tradition, no gospel of its own; it must nowhere seem, or in fact be, a foreign government."[31] That the universal government should have no moral tradition of its own seems to contradict the assertion on the very next page that "a universal government would have to be a particular government." Santayana appears to mean that, in order to rule other nations, a government must first have the integrity and the power that only an entrenched political organization can possess and that, secondly, it must be able to refrain from imposing its own traditions on subject peoples. For a nation to rule the world without being oppressive, it would have to lose its nationality and be reduced to the condition of the proletariat, of "the nondescript masses of human beings without country, religion, property, or skill."[32] It is true that we are all born physically alike, but this is the only sense in which Santayana grants that men are equal or human nature is proletarian. There is irony in his suggestion that "the Soviets might be better fitted than any other power to become the guardians of universal peace."[33] True, they are mighty and might conquer the world, and they could become neutral in matters of race, nationality, religion, and education. But in attaining neutrality they would lose their identity, and, therefore, they would lose the motive and power to rule. Furthermore, any government, to become universally successful and rational, would have to renounce all control of those institutions—language, religion, education, the arts—which are unique to each people and dominate its moral life. It is these which lift any nation above the status of proletarians, and it is these, too, which make foreign rule seem a domination to be overthrown. Here is a double irony, for it will become clear that, if they renounced control of the moral life, the Soviets would cease to govern at all, in the sense in which Santayana had come to understand government.

If there are no ultimate political ideals, neither is peace, in *Dominations and Powers,* prescribed as a universally desirable goal. Despite its "centrifugal" character, Santayana does not consider that the result of natural evolution would necessarily be total "war of all against all." On the other hand, he does not foresee increasing homogeneity or stability in human society, nor, in the end, does he regret this. In *Reason in Science* the germ of this position is already present, originating in the materialism on the basis of which that book develops a philosophy of physical, social, psychological, and moral science and of society. "The need of a material basis for spirit . . . renders partial war with parts of the world the inevitable background of charity and justice."[34] But here the moral idealism of *The Life of Reason* is manifest, for Santayana asserts that "the frontiers at which this warfare is waged may be pushed back indefinitely."[35] *Dominations and Powers* culminates in a discussion of the principles of a possible world government, but the uniqueness of societies takes precedence over their unification. Yet the degree to which the later work departs from the point of view of the earlier should not, in my opinion, be exaggerated. Even in writing *Reason in Science,* Santayana realized that social order evolves from diverse centers which are necessarily the basis of any further development. He had already formulated the contention of the later book that the scope of political order is necessarily limited, placing that limit at the point at which each nation would be unwilling to make any further concessions to any other. "Beyond or below that limit," he states there, "strife must continue for physical ascendancy" in order for the very power and will to be reasonable not to be undermined. For a nation that lost the will to retain its identity would cease to exist, and the organ of reason would have disappeared.[36]

A dominant note of Santayana's later criticism is "charity" to all forms of life. Charity, also a theme of *Reason in Religion,* is defined as justice to all impulses per se and identified with reason. *Dominations and Powers* emphasizes this and stresses, in addition to charity, appreciation of limited harmonies achieved and acceptance of inevitable frustration and conflict rather than insistence upon a greater accord than is typically possible. If value judgments and moral precepts are based on actual impulse and need, except from the point of view of a given individual there is no ground for preferring the good of one creature or group or species to that of any other; "wisdom lies not in pronouncing what sort of good is best but in understanding each good within the lives that enjoy it as it actually is in its physical complexion and in its moral essence."[37] Granted that the interest of the totality may in some sense outweigh, or at least must include, any individual interest, the total interest must still be defined. In *Dominations and Powers,* rejecting the possibility of a single collective interest, Santayana identifies the interest of the whole with the sum of individual interests. Ultimately, some interests must conflict, and mediation is often necessary. But unlike Spinoza and Hobbes, Santayana sees no necessity to strive for peace in general, perhaps because he sees that once society is established and custom prevails, anarchy is hardly a possibility. The value of peace depends on the price we must pay for it. And whereas "liberty habitually exercised presupposes peace; . . . the price of peace as men are actually constituted, is the suppression of almost all their liberties."[38] Santayana chooses liberty before peace. Distinctiveness, social cohesiveness, rooted in the dynamic and demanding psyche, inevitably result in war when individual areas of concern overlap. Dissociation is a kind of association, equally natural and inevitable. Being equally natural, war is neither more nor less rational than peace. Once individuality is construed to preclude unanimity, once the possibility of a universal human ideal is abandoned, the price of peace must be calculated anew for every instance of conflict. "There may be rational wars, as there are rational surgical operations. . . . The war will be rational, on one side or both, if the true interests of the nation would suffer more by avoiding it than by waging it."[39]

In *The Life of Reason,* though the benefits of competition are highly touted, the moral ramifications of war itself are more heavily weighed in its assessment: "the combative instinct is a savage prompting by which one man's good is found in another's evil. The existence of such a contradiction in the moral world is the original sin of nature, whence flows every moral wrong."[40] It is evident that Santayana sees, in the very nature of life itself and only thinly disguised by the veneer of culture, an impulse to destruction for its own sake, divorced from rational grounds. In *Dominations and Powers* it is reaffirmed even more strongly and viewed in a different moral light. Santayana describes "a sort of subterranean chaos, sometimes bursting through the crust of civilization. . . . a sort of self-hatred and self-contempt: a wild throw for something different, and a deep, dark impulse to challenge and to destroy everything that has the impertinence to exist."[41] Being primal and authoritative, this "death-instinct" must be recognized and may not be condemned.

Peace, if not stability, would be guaranteed if there were a universal human society or a total world-state. In *Dominations and Powers* such a monolith is not only impossible but undesirable. In the first place, men are motivated biologically, not rationally. Evolution is change, not necessarily progress, and movement is not always in a consistent direction. There is no natural development in the direction of one world, but rather "a compound of clashing endeavors and chequered fortunes."[42] In *Reason in Science* an ever more inclusive community is held to be made possible and desirable by natural sympathy. Sympathy and justice are assumed to be merely rational elaborations of Will. In *Dominations and Powers* the capacity for sympathy is nowhere denied, but its actualization is seen to be necessarily partial and fleeting. "A radical potentiality for sympathy with all virtues and all vices belongs to primal Will in every creature, but the direction and the degree in which such sympathy shall become actual is a question of contingent endowment and opportunity."[43] All motivation originates in the dynamic, self-perpetuating Will to dominate the environment and feed the self. The primary claim of life is absolute liberty; universal cooperation will never prevail. Sympathy is itself a function of inner direction and need, but because of the sheer existence of a multiplicity of dynamic centers, total community, a single society including all men, is precluded. The plurality of perspectives outweighs the generic similarity among individuals of the same species. Then, too, a perfect sympathy could only be adopted at the expense of personal integrity, and if universal sympathy destroyed preference or resulted in neurotic indecision, "we should no longer see any moral qualities or interests in the world, and history and politics would have ceased to exist for us."[44] By implication, it might be noted, mysticism, "spirituality" in the extreme sense, is also rejected.

Where real sympathy is not possible, "chivalry" may be: "a recognition of the inward right and justification of our enemies fighting against us."[45] But chivalry toward enemies does not eliminate war. And freedom to pursue naturally divergent ends involves the risk of conflict, a risk which Santayana holds nineteenth-century liberals did not sufficiently dignify. Even if universal sympathy were possible, it would involve the sacrifice of the very factors which have resulted in the greatest civilizations and cultural riches the world has known. Were we to give up our cherished idiosyncrasies, we would melt together in an indistinguishable mass. Whereas for the ideal detached observer, appreciation of all forms of community is the only just ethical stance, mutual toleration by those involved of all differences indiscriminately is impossible because of the existence of those very differences. Beneath all individual and cultural distinctiveness is the fact that each of us has a "Will" of his own to satisfy and a position of his own to defend. Perfect toleration, absolute forbearance, if forcibly imposed, will necessarily end in the annihilation of coherent society. Retain the pugnacious, exclusive individual (or, speaking metaphorically, group) Will, and conflict is inevitable. Suppress it, the only way to attain peace, and destroy not only all individuality, all tradition, but with them all personal and social identity and cohesiveness, personality and society themselves. This is the thinking behind Santayana's most disturbing criticism of the reforms necessary for the realization of the liberal ideal, for he believes the principle of equality to be based on the desire to attain peace at the price of racial identity. In the first place, he says, the liberal principle of toleration would not secure peace as long as differences prevailed. Secondly, if this policy did succeed in maintaining peace, it would do so only by the erosion of cultural differences and the disappearance of the distinct peoples. Tolerance and equality then would have led "to peace of the most radical kind, the peace of moral extinction. Between two nothings there is eternal peace; but between two somethings, if they come within range of each other, there is always danger of war."[46]

Santayana's faith in the eventual attainment of rationality in human life and society was never wholehearted. He could state, in *Reason in Common Sense,* that the life of reason is the result of natural tendencies; but in *Reason in Society* rationality is seen as a characteristic of only certain types of animal nature; it is a function of physiological factors which are not amenable to "education," to conscious appeal. Rationality is a rare occurrence: "people neither understand their own interests nor have the constancy to pursue them systematically."[47] Passion overcomes prudence, and private prudence does not always counsel what is also profitable to others; thus, reason is perpetually subject to defeat. "If reason were efficacious, kings might well be left to govern alone."[48] But though rational (i.e., compatible) interests occasionally predominate in a man or in a group, nature is more often brutal and people are self-centered. Furthermore, perfect rationality presupposes perfect self-knowledge, which is unattainable. Ultimately, Santayana held any thoroughgoing rational adjustment to be impossible in moral and political life. The possibility that reason may govern was very early taken to be "the babble of dreamers."[49] Political ideals, materialistically interpreted, are simply expressions of inner drives, unaware of circumstances and unrelated to one another. Underlying constitutional democracy (an important contemporary ideal held by many to be a rational adjustment to the diversity of interests in present-day life) is the assumption that man is fundamentally a reasoning animal who accepts the conclusions of logic in the course of discussion. Santayana would agree with Laski that "the history of government gives no ground for accepting the assumption as valid."[50]

With increasing disillusionment in regard to the possibility of reason triumphing in an irrational world, Santayana's conception of the nature of reason underwent a substantive change. Whereas in *The Life of Reason* the function of reason is to harmonize impulses in the light of an inclusive ideal of its own creation, in *Dominations and Powers* reason is no longer considered such a moral agency. Instead of a tendency to synthesize and to harmonize, it becomes simply "a faculty of seeing identity, affinity, contrast, or irrelevance between essences present together in direct intuition." Though applicable to "events and the whole history and composition of the world," reason is finally conceived as "purely speculative in itself."[51] This, of course, is like the late notion of spirituality. Santayana had earlier held that "speculative reason, if it is not also practical, is not reason at all."[52] The task of reason applied to action in *Reason in Common Sense* is that of "forming an ideal, so soon as the demands and satisfactions concerned are synthesized and balanced imaginatively."[53] The earlier view is that reason is essentially idealistic: "idealism is entrenched in the very structure of human reason," which is defined in *Reason in Common Sense* as "the gift of ideal construction and the aspiration toward eternal goods." Its aim is "that a harmony and cooperation of impulses should be conceived, leading to the maximum satisfaction possible in the whole community of spirits affected by our action."[54] Thus interpreted, reason is a factor making for wider social unity and mitigating difference and conflict. This tendency to unify, adjust, and harmonize is said to be the natural condition of mind. Reason here is thought to be prescriptive, to impose a distinctive method on all moral life by proposing ideals in which immediate ends are submerged and reconciled.

In *Dominations and Powers* reason is no longer permitted to formulate a moral ideal but is conceived to be morally neutral. Emanating from nature and depending on nature for its existence, reason "cannot rationally deny or condemn" any of the powers of nature. In addition, to the extent that spirit is "rational," it transcends any moral interest in nature. But spirit is said to be not completely rational: it "manifests an emotional and poetic sensibility which is not rational" and which renders its judgments irrational.[55] When it is rational, spirit does not take sides. But neither is it any longer an interest in reconciling conflict. In fact, it is no longer conceived to be an interest at all, as had been suggested in *Dialogues in Limbo,* where reason is said to be "like a dog that explores the road and all the by-ways when we walk abroad; but he cannot choose a direction or supply a motive for the journey, and we must whistle to him when we take a new turn."[56] In itself, reason is now seen as spectatorial. It is prepared to give free play to any and all interests able to prevail in the world. Thus, a rational ideal would be an ideal of freedom rather than of unification.

Reason can still explore the relations which obtain among the data of experience. In this capacity it may function in the service of a given ideal, and this ideal may itself be "rational" in the earlier sense of harmonizing existing interests. Furthermore, such an ideal may be espoused as a consequence of the consolidation of a personality or a group, the achievement of an inner harmony and strength which Santayana would consider to be itself rational. But he has come to believe that the desire to introduce any specific order into the world, to impose a given ideal rather than any other, is the result, not of reason, but of passion; it is an instance of what he calls "militancy." No matter how well-intentioned, well-informed, or unanimous the individual or party which wishes to impose a given order may be, that wish is an expression of interest, of commitment to the ideal itself, not of reason. Even a commitment to rationality is not rational but biological in origin.

Still, Santayana distinguishes in *Dominations and Powers* a "Rational Order of Society" from other political ideals, even those adopted by reflective and coherent parties. This order is no longer a "unity given to existence by a mind *in love with the good*."[57] A rational government, rather than seeking to impose a distinctive character on elements it desires to reconcile, will provide for the free development of all. As we shall see, Santayana believes that freedom presupposes discipline, and liberty and creativity can only flourish against a background of established tradition. Thus, he comes to the position that a rational order is possible only within a tightly managed society, where individuals have firm and coherent convictions and share the same heritage and outlook, insuring a minimum of distraction and internal conflict. If we are not to destroy civilization, we must permit societies to differ and, if necessary, to war. A rational society is one with a "strict and 'totalitarian' discipline" internally—like a monastery or a school or an army.[58] But the fact that any organization has the character it does is, of course, irrational, and each "race," having its own irrational core, will organize its rational development on a unique foundation. Thus, the possibility of peace among them would rest, first, on whether there were room and resources enough for them to coexist, and, second, on whether they were willing to do so. There would be no rational way to insure that willingness.

NOTES

[1] *RCS,* p. v.

[2] *RCS,* p. 6; p. 267.

[3] *Ibid.,* pp. v–vi.

[4] "Ideals and Essences in Santayana's Philosophy," in *Philosophy,* p. 187; cf. also pp. 206–13.

[5] *RR,* pp. 204–8.

[6] October 15, 1937. Reproduced in *The Journal of Philosophy*, LI, No. 2 (January 21, 1954), 55–56.

[7] *Philosophy*, pp. 3–30; passage cited, p. 27.

[8] *RCS*, p. 3.

[9] *RR*, p. 195.

[10] *Ibid.*, p. 196.

[11] *SE*, p. 167.

[12] *RR*, p. 212.

[13] *DP*, p. 427.

[14] *Ibid.*, p. 414.

[15] *RSci*, pp. 118–19.

[16] I say "an *increased* emphasis" on the diversity of human nature in view of Santayana's recognition, in the chapter entitled "Flux and Constancy in Human Nature" in *Reason in Common Sense*, of both the diversity and the variability of human nature.

[17] *RSci*, p. 238.

[18] Cf. *DP*, p. 362.

[19] *RCS*, p. 32.

[20] *SAF*, p. 45.

[21] *RCS*, p. vi.

[22] *DL*, p. 44.

[23] *DP*, p. vii.

[24] *RSci*, p. 245.

[25] *Letters*, pp. 416–17.

[26] *The Genteel Tradition at Bay* (New York: Charles Scribner's Sons, 1931), p. 65. Hereafter cited as *GTB*.

[27] *RCS*, p. 256.

[28] *Ibid.*, p. 23.

[29] *RSoc*, p. 173.

[30] *Ibid.*

[31] *DP*, p. 454.

[32] *Ibid.*, p. 455.

[33] *Ibid.*

[34] *RSci*, p. 236.

[35] *Ibid.*

[36] *Ibid.*, p. 237.

[37] *DP*, p. 466.

[38] *Ibid.*, p. 447.

[39] *Ibid.*, p. 439. It is interesting, in the light of their conflicting moral views, to compare this position with that of Kant: ". . . reason, from its throne of supreme moral legislating authority, absolutely condemns war as a

legal recourse and makes a state of peace a direct duty, even though peace cannot be established or secured except by a compact among nations." Immanuel Kant, *Perpetual Peace* (1795), Lewis White Beck, ed. and trans. (New York: The Library of Liberal Arts, 1957), p. 18.

[40] *RSoc*, p. 85.

[41] *DP*, pp. 439–40. Compare Kant again: ". . . nature guarantees perpetual peace by the mechanism of human passions. . . ." *Op. cit.*, p. 32.

[42] *DP*, p. 427.

[43] *DP*, p. 306.

[44] *Ibid.*, p. 198.

[45] *Winds of Doctrine* (New York: Charles Scribner's Sons, 1913; reprint: *Winds of Doctrine and Platonism and the Spiritual Life*, New York: Haper Torchbooks, 1957), p. 151.

[46] *DP*, p. 449.

[47] *RSoc*, p. 118.

[48] *Ibid.*

[49] *SE*, p. 104.

[50] Harold Laski, *Democracy in Crisis* (Chapel Hill, North Carolina: The University of North Carolina Press, 1933), p. 158.

[51] *DP*, p. 297.

[52] *RCS*, p. 176.

[53] *Ibid.*, p. 264.

[54] *Ibid.*, pp. 202–3.

[55] *DP*, p. 298.

[56] *DL*, pp. 225–26.

[57] *RCS*, p. 46.

[58] *DP*, p. 296.

CHAPTER 7

Militancy and the Moral Life

THE CATEGOREAL SCHEME of *Reason in Society* is paralleled, but not duplicated, by the tripartite organization of *Dominations and Powers,* where Santayana describes the social process in terms of three "orders": the "generative," the "militant," and the "rational." The two sets of categories represent different approaches to the analysis of social institutions and societal ideals. The earlier work portrays the life of man in relation to three different kinds of society, a society being understood as an assemblage of persons or symbols ("personages") to which men have functional and meaningful relations. The major categories of *Dominations and Powers,* on the other hand, stand for constellations of "powers," social forces which (1) establish, preserve, and enforce customs, laws, and sanctions and govern the nurture and socialization of the young (the generative order); (2) stubbornly introduce changes in the habitual or traditional order of nature or society or attempt to prevail in disregard of instinctive movements (the militant order); or (3) provide for the intrinsically rewarding employment of human effort (the rational order).

Despite the fact that these categories are superimposed on a lengthy, rambling book which was written piecemeal over a long period, the terms are systematically interconnected and emphasize recurrent themes in Santayana's social and political thought. The underlying unity of *Dominations and Powers,* like that of *The Life of Reason,* is provided by Santayana's metaphysical and moral naturalism. Partly because of the circumstances of its composition and partly because of the inconsistencies in Santayana's metaphysics, this late work is not without contradictions. Nor is it free of factual error or prejudice. Santayana was neither a political scientist nor an "expert" in worldly affairs. His political statements do not reflect a consistent identification with any school of political thought; their very idiosyncrasy is one of the things that make them of interest. *Dominations and Powers* is not a narrowly political treatise; like the rest of Santayana's work, it focusses on basic philosophic categories.

The substance of the book is buried in a prodigious mass of seemingly casual, and not always consecutive, commentary and allegory. But in many ways it is a summary volume, representative of its author's perennial interests and increasingly detached vision. I have undertaken the reconstruction of certain aspects of this work so as to exhibit more clearly the principles of his mature philosophy of society. The theme of *Dominations and Powers* is the tension between Santayana's conviction that men should be free and the knowledge that they must be governed.[1] The necessity of government is ontological, not merely moral: like every determinate form of life, Santayana believes, society arises spontaneously but functions restrictively. "Society suffocates liberty merely by existing, and it must exist, and all its members are equally its slaves."[2] The very powers which give birth to the individual, which care for him and prepare him to take his place among them, are dominations which restrict his freedom and oppress his spirit. His relations to parents, to society itself, to the customs by which it rules itself and him, are forms of "necessary servitude."[3] In a more obvious way government, too, must dominate in order to benefit.

The generative order, the order of nature, is at one and the same time the sphere of spontaneity and constraint. Comprising those powers and dominations without which the individual could not exist and which have the most profound influence on his development, it includes "natural society" but involves several distinctions that extend its scope beyond that of the earlier category. Both natural society and the generative order of society may be interpreted as analyses of the "natural basis" of society which projects and conditions its "ideal development."[4] Both analyses articulate Santayana's materialist assumptions and exemplify the conception of matter as the dynamic and fertile source of all worth and all meaning. As George H. Sabine noted in reviewing *Dominations and Powers,* the distinction between existence and essence—the most characteristic feature of Santayana's metaphysics—has considerable import for his politics.[5] Sabine also noted the evident connection between Santayana's doctrine and Schopenhauer's distinction between Will and Idea. Santayana takes Schopenhauer's category of "Will" to be a psychological name for "matter," "energy," or "movement," all of which are, for Santayana, names for "the true process of universal genesis."[6] The generative order of society is said by Santayana to be an embodiment of Will; its constituents are organisms governed by the principles which govern all matter. Schopenhauer's "great intuition, the cornerstone of his philosophy," which is also Santayana's fundamental thesis, "was precisely the priority of automatism and instinct over the intellect."[7]

Santayana distinguishes events which arise "by involuntary growth" from those stemming from "militant or rational action," but all these are species of one genus, and all events are held by him to arise according to the generative order of nature.[8] Spontaneous social relations, generated out of impulse and need, harden into customs, and the fundamental order of any society is traditional. It is important for him that it is institutions, rather than private sentiment alone, which make societies conservative. And these very institutions, by their rise, make civilization and culture possible. The generative order of society is both creative and coercive, a system of constraints which, just by limiting freedom, determines the specific directions in which freedom can be realized. Santayana's opposition to liberalism stems, in part, from this principle: the official liberal doctrine is to introduce restraint only where freedom of one sort would interfere with other freedoms. Santayana points out that specific freedoms are determined by specific limitations. In addition, he notes that a society which did not define the freedoms it permits could not exist. And, in fact, he holds liberal practice to involve the prescription of a distinctive way of life with a characteristic Protestant bias.[9]

While it is continuous with nature at large, the generative order of society is distinct from sheer physical existence, the realm of matter, which nevertheless underlies and constitutes it. Intrinsically, all power is physical, but society has a political, and not simply a natural, life. "Political" in this context is used by Santayana to mean "pertaining to *policy*" and not specifically to "polity." Organisms become political—Santayana seems to mean they become *persons*—when they act on and become aware of their motives, and this occurs only in society. "Physical powers . . . begin to figure in politics only when they are exercised by persons forming a society, or capable of forming one."[10] The purely automatic activity that characterizes much of animal life cannot be called political; political life involves conscious pursuit of policies, principles, or ideologies. The political domain is therefore a moral domain. All animals are possessed of impulses and instincts, but only a social animal judges others, seeing them as if they wore masks expressive of their political or moral character.[11] The behavior of a herd is not truly social in that it is not political. Animals instinctively travel together, mate, rear their young as far as necessary, and fight; men, once they are accustomed to living according to policies, rules, and laws, react to the policies they discern in the behavior of others, acting politically in return and becoming simultaneously aware of their own and others' images. Accompanying this awareness are self-conscious competition and deliberate conflict as well as many forms of social organization. "Psyches, or forms of life, bear no hatred or ill-will towards other psyches; they simply have no imagination, until they develop a highly social and cooperative way of living."[12]

Action which is "political" in this sense belongs to the militant order of society. The term "militancy," as Santayana uses it in *Dominations and*

Powers, is a metaphor standing for the stubbornness of the human Will that is responsible for both innovation and political domination. This concept would seem to be an elaboration of the notion of political society implicit in *Reason in Society* and discussed in Chapter IV above. It has been distorted by Santayana's interpreters, and its import has not been appreciated, with the result that much of what he says in *Dominations and Powers* has been misconstrued. The source of militancy is the blind willfulness of the living animal, the elemental spontaneity of the organism; thus, it is said to be "a strand in the generative order."[13] But militancy is not just initiatory activity; a Will become militant is one which *adheres to a fixed aim,* sometimes in disregard of the conditions of its realization. Militancy in any sphere may extend, change, or complicate the existing scheme of things by deliberate innovation; alternatively, it may persist arbitrarily and fanatically in a mode of behavior or a course of action. In some cases a militant Will overrides the claims of others, and at such times it is tyrannical. But in other cases it makes for progress and may even contribute to the resolution of conflict.

Militancy is not necessarily evil or dangerous: Santayana says, for example, "The militancy of trade and of political reform seemed vital and almost normal, and undoubtedly it lent a speed and brilliancy to the growth of industry and of wealth in the nineteenth century which seemed to contemporaries an unmixed good, to be pursued and intensified for ever."[14] Intrinsically, like all natural tendencies, militancy involves the pursuit of an ideal and, to those who share it, this ideal is a good. But, despite the fact that militancy as defined is morally neutral, Santayana often condemns its manifestations. The language he employs in talking about militancy frequently seems expressive of an aesthetic or moral bias (as against a theoretical commitment) which may be relevant to specific contexts rather than to the presence of militancy per se. Often it is plainly inconsistent with the general concept.

Militancy is decidedly not to be equated with war, as Lamprecht and others have supposed.[15] In fact, not all wars are militant, on Santayana's usage, only those which are initiated in the express interest of dominating another people. "Even destruction, even war, is not always inspired by a militant spirit or meant to impose a domination; it may be unintended destruction or purely defensive and unwelcome war."[16] Neither spontaneous nor accidental conflict nor simple altercation is militant, no matter how much spoliation it may cause. "Existence itself, since it involves continual lapse and renewal of forms and relations, is essentially a blind and involuntary war," but natural growth and competition are still "innocent."[17] Conflict is only called militant when it is "intentional, self-righteous, and fanatical," when an aggressive power "thirsts to destroy its enemies and to see nothing in the world except its own likeness."[18] This is an instance of the pejorative use of "militancy" to which I have called attention.

Santayana says of militancy that "it is blind to its own accidental bias and to the equal legitimacy of all existence."[19] But he takes this to be equally true of the participants in the "universal passive war" which is the life of nature. It is only when a psyche knowingly wishes to make over the world in its own interest and at the expense of competing interests that it is said to be militant. But if, as Santayana holds, awareness is only the reflection of psychic tendencies, one may ask if there is any effective difference between a psyche which blindly destroys everything in its path and one which does so while conscious of an intent to destroy.

"Wars of growth" are not militant. "Wars of imagination," inspired by the intention to conquer another people or to convert them to one's own way of life, are. Missionaries and politicians, suffragettes and the Women's Christian Temperance Union, even pacifists, are militant. Patriotism is militant when it is a "political passion" rather than an "ideal allegiance." Each of these instances of militancy is distinguished by an effort to direct the course of events rather than follow an established regularity of nature. The militant order of society might be termed the order instituted specifically by *initiative*. "Enterprise," as well as "faction," is militant. Enterprise is militant in so far as it undertakes to change the circumstances of economic life. Mere industry, in contrast, simply takes advantage of circumstances and assists nature, as in agriculture, to bring forth its fruits. A stoic conformity to nature would be rational; the enterprising effort to "dominate" nature (which Santayana points out can only be accomplished by conforming at a deeper level) is militant, and each may be beneficial in its own way.

In addition to economic and specifically political militancy, there may be militancy in morality, in religion, and even in inquiry. Religion, when it congeals into dogma and ritual and these are held to be necessary for personal and social welfare, has become political. Actually, Santayana takes the spheres of institutional religion and government to be identical; thus, a "true" religion would be coincident with wise legislation and rational government. In becoming political, therefore, religion does not necessarily become objectionable. The Hindu, Jewish, Catholic, and Mohammedan religions are all militant in this sense, even without meddling in the technical affairs of state. A religious sect is militant in another direction and is not rational when it imposes its practices and beliefs upon groups of people to whom they are not native; again, religion is militant when it is set up in competition with science and when its doctrines, which are mythical, are taken to be literally true of nature.

Being voluntary, the militant order of society might be thought to be the equivalent of free society as described in *Reason in Society*. But the militant order of society is not an association of persons. It is the "artificial" perpetuation or deliberate transformation of an existing social order. Militant social change may be sudden and dramatic, as in political revolutions, or gradual, as in the case of the industrial revolution, but the latter was nevertheless a product of initiative and therefore of militancy. Neither social change nor reaction need be violent to be militant. In either case, the element of militancy lies in the persistent effort to redirect an ongoing social process.

According to Santayana's mechanistic materialism and epiphenomenalism, what we call intent is the expression of automatic processes. If this is so, militancy can only be understood to be voluntary, or deliberate, in a qualified sense. To be voluntary, for Santayana, is to be an act of Will. "Will" in this context is more than simple automatism. It is power organized in such a way as to achieve a result toward which it appears to be *directed.* Thus, Santayana denies that plants have Will on the grounds that they do not show any "eagerness to act" or any "sense of urgency."[20] But such a sense, on his theory, would have to be an accompaniment or an appearance of the physical processes involved in an act and could not be their cause. Furthermore, he denies that consciousness is essential to Will. Foreseeing and desiring an end is called "will," with a small letter, and is not identified with the dynamism of action.[21] Primal Will is a complication of automatism, which "always envelops and subtends it," but the difference between the two is mysterious, and it is hard for me to see how they could be differentiated on purely physical grounds.

That an act is voluntary, according to Santayana, does not imply intelligence, premeditation, or any previous idea of its object or its result. Initiative is conceived by him to be the action of the psyche, the "hidden self" which, like any power, is part of the general movement of nature. Rather than being the product of conscious deliberation, voluntary action is taken to be biologically determined. Internally it does not seem to differ from automatism. The only way Santayana distinguishes it from other forces seems to be in the way it is viewed in relation to them. Militancy, a modification of Will, is said to be "a strand in the generative order of society, an eddy in the stream, when one vital interest becomes vivid and turns against the smothering pressure of the undirected flow of events." It is simply "the integrity of a part asserting itself and seeking to dominate the blind drift of the rest."[22] Unless consciousness is taken to be efficacious, "directing" events and "seeking" to dominate must be understood behavioristically. According to this behaviorist interpretation, the defining characteristic of "militancy" would be divergence from the dominant course of events, rather than the *wish* to divert the course of nature or history. This is consistent with Santayana's thesis, but the problem remains, I think, of distinguishing between simple divergence and "militant" divergence. Construing militancy in this way makes the concept of "Will" even more problematic. How would Santayana distinguish between voluntary and involuntary *conformity*?

In so far as it is in harmony with some "deeper" current preparing for change, militant action (which is, after all, the operation of a natural power) may successfully modify a prevalent tendency. To the extent that it *is* thus in "harmony" with natural powers, Santayana would call it "rational." But militancy, while it may occasionally coincide with rationality, differs from the latter. Rationality is harmony with or conformity to "circumstances"; militancy is the attempt to oppose or alter them. The two may overlap, but the same action would be militant in one perspective and rational in another. Santayana explicitly points out that the orders of society are not to be thought of as mutually exclusive.[23] Thus, the fact that militancy may have a rational aspect, or vice versa, presents no special problem.

It may be observed here that the three orders of society in a certain respect reduce to one, the generative order. Santayana distinguishes them by pointing out that the militant and rational orders denote distinct types of conditions brought about by the interplay of natural powers. The "generative" order is well named: it generates the other two and provides the motive force in each. The distinction among the orders is not an ontological separation, as is the distinction between existence and essence, any more than it is a distinction of separate natural processes. Like that between dominations and powers, it is a *moral* distinction, made "in view of the different *moral results* generated by the concourse of all natural forces."[24]

Any attempt to change an existing order or frustrate a prevalent tendency, whether successful or not, would be classified by Santayana as militant. When a course of action is not in any way supported by circumstances, when it runs strongly counter to the spontaneous course of events, militancy is futile. It is still part of the generative order of nature, but there is a sense in which Santayana says that the effort to control natural processes, "to dominate matter materially," is "contrary to nature." He grants that this can sometimes be accomplished, but not with any lasting effect.[25] Militancy in politics, for instance, is generally fruitless, for traditions are deeply embedded in the social fabric and are automatically efficacious. Innovation in art or industry, since it is embodied in a physical product, can endure even though men go back to old ways of doing things. But the material of politics is the human Will: any attempt to establish a social system can succeed only to the extent that psyches are made to act in unison, and established habits are much more likely to prevail than are novel policies, however spectacularly introduced. "An artificial morality strains the heart and rends the world, and the majority always hates it."[26]

Both reactionaries and revolutionaries are intent on imposing upon others a social order of their own design to which they cling regardless of its feasibility and regardless of the various and changing needs of men. They are each in love with an ideal and are equally militant and equally fanatical. A fanatic, Santayana points out, disregards existent conditions in favor of utopian ends; he would like to coerce the Will of others for his own purposes and may be so intent upon his end that he believes the means to it exist in the world when they do not. Thus, "the fanatic is a tyrant on principle and often a hypocrite in practice."[27] The major weapon of fanatics is propaganda, which Santayana defines as "intentionally controlling the movement of ideas by social agencies."[28] Of course, for a materialist, it is not ideas but the "contagious" movement of the psyche in their adoption that is effective. "In a biological view the agencies that control ideas are always ultimately physical: human nature, race, environment, and the balance of passions and employments in particular men."[29] Propaganda is used by conservatives to inspire horror for new ideas and to revive old allegiances; revolutionaries use it to discredit tradition. In either context Santayana contends that propaganda is "artificial": because it is an attempt to instill a different and often unwelcome viewpoint, it flouts "natural" tendencies and subverts native ideals. The attempt to maintain the status quo in the face of strong progressive tendencies would be, according to this interpretation, as militant and as artificial as the efforts at reform which he takes to be militancy *in excelsis,* and it would be equally a domination.

Significantly, on this view, to espouse any ideology is to be militant. For Santayana no genuine ideal would be absolutely wrong, and, therefore, none can legitimately be held to be absolutely right. But all political ideologies, he says, are attempts to impose private opinions uniformly on the public and produce an artificial unanimity by suppressing divergent movements. Furthermore, an ideology or political dogma, besides being partial and biased, entails a presumption that men will not change. It prescribes the course of history, rather than following the generative order of nature, and often is associated with insistence upon a course of action without regard for actual needs or effective natural opposition. Commitment to an ideology is then idolatrous since it elevates a means to the status of an end.

This is not to say that Santayana claims that political ideals are altogether expendable. Good government, he says, must be justified by a view of an "ideal economy," by a proper conception of the balance between order and liberty and of the "ultimate" welfare of its subjects.[30] But the ideal he has in view is one which, unlike those of ideological sects, would encourage, rather than transform or overthrow, separate local and national economies and would preserve, rather than destroy or modify, traditions.

Liberalism, according to this conception, is a militant ideology actually committed to an ideal of unanimity and universal cooperativeness which, Santayana holds, disregards natural differences. If this ideal could be attained, it would be at the expense of existing individuality and traditional distinctiveness. Santayana claims that liberals overestimate the uniformity of real interests among men, and attribute to all only the desire for material comfort and personal liberty. In so doing, he believes, they ignore the whole spectrum of values to which men are committed. Liberals assert, furthermore, that both wealth and liberty can be achieved through political and economic democracy, whereas Santayana charges that the latter is inimical to genuine freedom. Liberals are "dogmatists who when in power think they are ruling for the good of mankind."[31] The fault he finds with them is that they prejudge that good and foist their own values on everyone. Not that men always and everywhere can be trusted to know their own good: it is a principle of Santayana's that self-government is not necessarily good government; good government presupposes deep knowledge of the needs of the governed, a knowledge which is to be attained only by a combination of sensitivity and science. "It is knowledge and knowledge only that may rule by divine right, no matter who possesses that knowledge and, possessing it, gives the word of command."[32]

But Santayana also holds that good government must be "morally representative," that is, it must foster the diverse natural groupings present in society and cherish, not obliterate (as he claims liberals would), their heterogeneous ideals. A moral representative, as opposed to a political representative or to a merely typical individual, "would have to appreciate justly all the people's interests and to know, at the same time, which interests and how far each of those interests could be successfully served at the moment."[33] He must not necessarily resemble, nor need he be chosen by, those whom he would represent: the element of moral representation lies in furthering the interests of the governed, not in winning their votes. There is an important difference, too, between a representative who speaks for the interests of a people, which are variable, and one who promulgates what Santayana would take to be an ideological myth and tries to enact it permanently into reality. Moral representation is related to rational ethics as described in *Reason in Science* and is based on a "dialectical" analysis of intent. The moral representative must constantly apply the Socratic maxim to the interests he would further. "It must be therefore in the Will of the people, not of the government, that the criterion must be found for determining the true good of that people."[34] That good is to be established scientifically and not, as the democrats hold, by bargaining. Santayana distinguishes sharply between Will and consciousness, between nature and desire. The good proper to any creature is a function of the demands and potentialities of his nature or "Will," not of his conscious wishes or "will." To strive to fulfill desires, rather than fundamental needs and capacities, would be militant, for, rather than trying to perceive the inevitable direction of nature, consciousness would thus dictate to nature what its good is to be.

In order to be morally representative, Santayana points out, a delegate must be a moral agent in his own right. Government is an art, and "the most impersonal and disinterested arts are also arts of self-expression."[35] To be effective, government must have an ethical position of its own, for a ruler who lacked commitment could hardly act at all. In the absence of conviction, too, a person would merely vacillate and become an agent of others with the strength of their own convictions, as is the case with politicians whose only interest is to remain in office and whose policies become those of the powers that keep them there. A benevolent desire to rule in the interest of the governed is inadequate to insure representative government. A good ruler, Santayana asserts, must have in addition to this vague desire the wisdom and integrity to give direction and the energy to do so successfully. The ideal ruler would have to be animated by the real interest of the people, which he would have to comprehend as the people themselves in their impulsive and short-sighted militancy cannot, and which he would forward with an eye to the powers that might frustrate or encourage the realization of the people's good. The latter requirement is the essence of rationality as it is delineated in *Dominations and Powers*. That such a moral scientist may not exist does not, for Santayana, make him less needed. But most politicians are devoted only to pleasing people, and the rest are militant idealists intent upon converting them.

The judgment that ideologies are egotistical appears to be a rejection of moral idealism. According to Santayana, the advocacy of any utopian ideal is a militant rebellion against nature, "for what is the motive power in militancy? The Will of an individual or a group diverging from the wider automatic course of nature, and attempting to transform it to suit that group or that individual."[36] But if a Utopian ideal is militant, organized opposition to it, in proposing its own ideology, is similarly militant and equally futile. The older Santayana feels that tradition and entrenched morality will eventually defeat any attempt to deliberately institute or reconstruct a given social order, and spontaneous movements will overcome attempts to resuscitate a dying tradition. Santayana does not condemn militancy wholesale, yet it is clear that he considers most militant political efforts foolhardy, and in this is a true conservative, not on moral, but on metaphysical (or "physical") grounds. "Man is a part of nature and his militant intervention does not in the least disturb the broad order of generation in the universe."[37]

In the light of its appeal to the generative order of nature for the standard to be employed in the assessment of political action, Santayana's conservatism is more aptly called "political naturalism." In his review of *Dominations and Powers* Sabine points out:

Mr. Santayana's political philosophy belongs to a type more common in the seventeenth and eighteenth centuries than in the nineteenth and twentieth. It turns upon the ancient distinction between "nature" and artifice and seeks in the former a criterion by which present change might be moderated, destructive forces controlled, and fundamental values discriminated and safeguarded.[38]

I believe Sabine to have misinterpreted Santayana to this extent: the choice of "nature" as a criterion does not seem to have been dictated by Santayana's concern to moderate change and control destructive forces or to safeguard any particular set of values he considers fundamental. In *Dominations and Powers* he is nearly equally disdainful of all worldly aims and all contemporary civilizations. For the most part the book seems to illustrate his claim that in the moral light in which he is accustomed to seeing the world, every form of organization can be found to have its own worth and its own interest, "and the Power or Domination that roots out one beauty, plants another; so that through the tears of the historian there often comes a smile, and the evening of one civilisation is the morning of another."[39] Santayana himself can approve any power that is strong enough to prevail—even when that power is a domination.

I do not believe, either, that the appeal to nature is made on the grounds that the natural is morally better than the artificial, but simply on the basis of his conviction that the inertia of physical and biological nature *will* prevail and is in the end the real ruler. Political phenomena are, to him, "physical fatalities," intrinsically neither good nor bad, products of "circumstantial pressures" by which "everybody is drawn into courses which no one has freely chosen."[40] Circumstances are tyrannical. If he understands this, an intelligent individual can become a successful tyrant, Santayana says, citing Lenin as an example; such a person reads the signs of the times and jumps into the breach, an action which can only count as rational.

But that the natural, if that word denotes the actual or the existent, is not necessarily to be taken as the good, is implied by Santayana's lifelong doctrine of the function of ideals. Everything existing has its *ideal* realization, its proper perfection, and it is not simply what exists that is good. The standard of true virtue, he says, is "what is *naturally* admirable and splendid."[41] He rejects the notion that everything that manages to achieve ascendance is good: by "naturally admirable," he asserts, he does not mean simply "prevalent in the animal kingdom" or even "producing some good results," for nearly everything has some good result. By "naturally admirable" he claims to mean what an interested person *judges* to be admirable. But not any judgment merely as such is a satisfactory criterion of value. In the first place, Santayana specifies that the judge of what is worthy in any realm must be experienced. Secondly, he asserts that the ultimate standard of value is to be provided by human nature as it is represented in the judge. But the actual nature of the judge is not acceptable; the only adequate criterion of judgment is an ideal of himself "as he would be happy in being; and the value he sets on things must be such as he would set upon them with full knowledge both of them and of himself."[42] This, I believe, is manifestly an unattainable standard. And Santayana is not consistent in placing the criterion of excellence anywhere but in sheer ascendancy.

The problem for the ethical naturalist is to establish standards of value and moral criteria without violating his naturalism. To deny that whatever is, is good, is necessarily to set up a standard which, in its partiality, seems to depart from nature itself as the standard of values. Santayana resolves this difficulty by asserting that nature (the ultimate power) does, in fact, give rise to ideals and generate standards of value. Men do adopt goals, make choices, espouse beliefs, and develop tastes. To the degree that these reflect the real interests of their authors these judgments are to be accepted as defining legitimate values (omitting for the moment the question of the possibility of attaining them). When value judgments conflict, however, we are constrained to ask what we really want. This question can be answered "rationally," according to Santayana, in the light of knowledge of what our own nature and circumstances permit. Granted that one eventuality is more likely than others, and that some things are impossible, we would still not always want to settle for what is attainable, and Santayana insists that this refusal itself is, when dictated by deep inner promptings, no violation of the naturalist position since preference, even a preference for rationality, is itself natural. A moral naturalism must not, as he sees it, degenerate into romanticism, the indiscriminate love of anybody or of any ideals. To be just, to recognize the claim of every form of life to light and air, is not to be morally dead. To exist, he had said in *The Genteel Tradition at Bay,* is to be distinct; therefore, universal toleration "sins against the principle of life itself." The price of relinquishing one's biases, he said there, would be to "sink into moral anarchy and artistic impotence—the very things from which our liberal, romantic world is so greatly suffering."[43] Despite this growing emphasis on impartiality, Santayana continues in *Dominations and Powers* to value cultural uniqueness and personal and social distinction, which he takes to be consequent upon coherent organization and firmly established traditions (themselves stemming ultimately from the spontaneous life of "psyche" and its adjustment to "circumstances"). A characteristic of his conservatism is his insistence on the preservation of tradition—not all traditions, nor any particular tradition, but tradition per se—partly on the ground that its abandonment would lead to disorder. In the absence of tradition and custom, he claims that law would be ineffectual; overt government would be impossible without tacit acceptance of the customs and institutions by which people actually are ruled. But because of his "biological" approach to society, and its corollary individualism, Santayana does not accept social order as the primary desideratum in precisely the same way as most conservatives do. One of the fundamental theorems of his philosophy of society is that custom and tradition are two-faced, that they are restrictive: just in so far as they constrict the spontaneous psyche they are dominations, and defense of them is in some sense militant. He sees militant rebellion, however, to be destructive and self-defeating since it usually brings about a new domination, even though genuine reform would establish a more satisfying social order. He takes particular traditions to be justified pragmatically. Like the assumptions of common sense or of science, he contends, they have proved useful in enabling life to go on, and there is consequently a presumption in their favor. Yet, for him, any convention is to some extent arbitrary, and a prescribed mode of behavior cannot be taken to be right just because it is conventional: that would be moral absolutism.[44] One may ask whether Santayana's presumption in favor of established tradition is not also absolutist since he neglects to ask whether a different tradition, a different set of customs, might not have made life in a given society *better.*

Conservatism is characterized by respect for authority. Sabine interprets Santayana's admiration for monarchical government as an expression of approval of a patriarchal form of "political control."[45] I believe a better and important insight into this political philosophy is gained if we recognize that by "authority" Santayana does not mean political, but *natural,* control. The "two authorities" which he asserts, in *Dominations and Powers,* must govern behavior if it is to be rational are "the *authority of things,* that permit, prevent, reward, or punish our actions; and *the authority of primal Will* within us, that chooses our path and discriminates between success and disaster in our careers."[46] This is, as we shall see, a fundamental doctrine. Santayana does not call for obedience simply to authorities, political, religious, or intellectual. Under the rubric of "rational authority," which can be defined as the authority of *nature,* he includes the established system of social norms among the "circumstances" which men must respect in order to carry out any policies successfully; but circumstances, for him, are far more comprehensive. And the actual drives and real needs of men are also, according to him, authorities to be taken into account. If Santayana's claim were that nature is ipso facto authoritative, a critic might charge that his doctrine is empty; but this is not the case. Santayana's concept of natural authority is grounded on the thesis that the dynamism of Will or psyche is the ultimate source of value. "Fact or Power, taken absolutely, contain no authority. Authority is a relation; and it accrues to a fact, a power, or an idea when any one of these is found to confront, or inwardly to control, the satisfaction of primal Will."[47] *Rationality* now consists in the perpetual adjustment of the two naturally authoritative factors, one internal to, one outside, the individual. The duality of rational authority must not be overlooked, despite Santayana's Stoic bias, for he holds that compromise with circumstances is not always desirable. It must always be weighed against the values whose sacrifice it involves, values which represent natural instincts and accumulated traditions.

In *Dominations and Powers* Santayana rejects even rationality as an absolute good or end in itself, although he recommends it as a practical standard. There are times when we cannot, or will not, abandon a personal goal in favor of a more rational ideal, for to do so would be to violate our integrity to an intolerable degree. When we are disillusioned with what we can attain in this world we still try to imagine the fulfillment of our desires and the attainment of the ideals which epitomize for us our own best nature. The sphere of such "potential goods," however, when they are not attainable, is no longer the sphere of politics as Santayana sees it, but that of post-rational morality and religion, removed from the sphere of rational action. The import of Santayana's mature political philosophy is that there can be no absolute moral values. The only legitimate ends are those freely adopted by living creatures, who only occasionally choose to be rational and often find rational values unacceptable. Devotion to ideals *as such* is outside the realm of rationality and is militant because commitment overrides considerations of practicality or natural tendency. But because it arises when the self is well integrated, Santayana sees allegiance to an ideal to be healthy. In the end, it is for him the only way to redeem life from vanity, the only salvation for the human soul, and the only ultimate freedom.

I do not think Santayana's doctrine is that authority is to be respected because it is requisite for the maintenance of order. Rather, authority *exists*, and we must recognize it, for we ignore it at our peril. Sabine interprets Santayana's attitude toward monarchy and patriarchy as a desire to replace anarchy with authority.[48] While I would not deny the contention that Santayana's intent is to reinforce order and strengthen authority, I believe Sabine's interpretation fails to do justice to the fact that Santayana portrays patriarchy as the model, not of authority in the traditional sense, but of moral representation. He conceives the legitimacy of a government to be a function neither of its history nor of the consent of the governed, but of its representativeness. Like a good father, an ideal ruler would appreciate and sympathize with the aims and potentialities of his people and discover the best way to their greatest possible fulfillment. "Monarchy" is ideal for Santayana in another sense as well: government, being an art, can only be carried on by a single Will. Therefore, all real government would have to be monarchical or unitary.[49]

In *Dominations and Powers* Santayana takes issue with some of the political views to which he himself had applied the term "political naturalism" in *The Genteel Tradition at Bay*.[50] There he had praised the politics of Carthage and Sparta, the Soviets, and the Italian Fascists, as well as the political philosophies of Bacon and Machiavelli, all of which he termed naturalistic. What they have in common is a highly determinate internal order (or the prescription of such an order) and an intense commitment, both of which, when their source is within the body politic, he took to be indices of health and of strength, and therefore criteria of political morality. He never disavowed the criteria. But he came to believe that the Communists would impose an artificial unanimity by extinguishing all contrary tendencies, while he continued to think that both the Church and the nationalist movements were among the powerful and indigenous developments of the generative order of society, representing real human needs and therefore not militant dominations. That for so long he did not recognize in Fascism a militant effort to suppress forces which were just as legitimate as those pressing for national order, that he failed to notice that this order was externally enforced and not exuberantly adopted, is hard to explain. It might be noted that it is an error he shared with many eminent scholars. Santayana's prejudice (which I believe to be one with his general aristocratic bias) and his ignorance of actual events are unquestionable and inexcusable. The principle at issue, a crucial axiom of Santayana's moral naturalism, remains worthy of consideration: the integrity of a coherent and healthy organism (or society) must be respected. This principle, dangerously close to a principle of natural moral selection, is fundamental to his conception of a rational order of society. The application of the principle is a separate issue, and there is some evidence that toward the end of his life Santayana interpreted authoritarianism somewhat differently. In a passage in *Dominations and Powers* the Pope and the nationalist dictators are characterized as autocrats, militantly trying to impose on the world their own conceptions of its welfare. To accomplish this, Santayana here contends, would require the sacrifice of the native ambitions of the various peoples of the world to a "higher" but oppressive ideal. To submit to such a regime, he says, would be martyrdom and "collective suicide."[51]

Correcting Machiavelli in *Dominations and Powers,* Santayana charges that the Machiavellian view involves a confusion between the efficacy of means and the choice of ends. Santayana considers the determination of ends to be the sole moral act; means are to be evaluated only in terms of the ends toward which they are directed. Machiavelli holds that a ruler who wishes to remain in power must do as others do and beat them at their own game. To do so is politically right just because it has always been done. Santayana considers this false morality. Just to remain in power, merely to survive, is not a legitimate goal for a moral creature, only a means to an end. Machiavelli and more recent practitioners of *Realpolitik* have assumed, says Santayana, that the Will to Live is the dominant moral force and the Will to remain in power is the sole political motive. But governments and states, as well as men, are mortal; simply to survive is the goal of brutes who are incapable of recognizing the ephemeral character of existing beings. The only truly human and civilized goal, whether for a private individual or a ruler, is not just to live but somehow to make this life worthwhile, "to redeem human life from vanity and barbarism" even at the expense of one's own life.[52] We may ask whether this is a naturalistic or simply an aristocratic judgment. Santayana here is trying to reconcile his naturalism with moral idealism; his argument is as follows: if men could live forever, then the desire to do so would be appropriate and rational. Since they cannot, the dialectic which exhibits true needs and exposes those which are in conflict or are unrealizable shows us that men's good lies elsewhere—in the attempt to realize as much that is really valuable to them as possible. The natural and proper basis of political morality is provided by men's specific aspirations for themselves. These must be based on adequate knowledge of the possibilities of their own constitutions and of the world. On the grounds of his own understanding of human nature, Santayana judges that the highest good for a man is in contemplation of the ideal, in spiritual freedom.

According to Santayana's political morality, the more immediate ends men choose for themselves may not be generalized. Only to the extent that people are really alike can they be said to have a common good, and this is a factual question not to be decided a priori. Nor are human values to be attributed to the universe.[53] To do so is the kind of error Santayana calls "egotism." Egotism is defined in *Egotism in German Philosophy* as "subjectivity in thought and wilfulness in morals."[54] The same notion is carried over into *Dominations and Powers,* where egotism is said to be a species of militancy, a kind of inertia of primal Will. The underlying drive in all human (as in all animal) behavior is there taken to be blind initiative, the stubborn urge to act, deeper in us than chastening experience can penetrate and reflected in our thoughts. "Like the hidden fires of a volcano, ignorant energy, convinced of its own rightness, will burst spasmodically into civil and rational life." The assumption of the efficacy, or even the literal truth, of thoughts in either political or intellectual contexts Santayana calls egotism and holds to dominate modern philosophy as well as politics.[55] Egotism is a chronic militancy of the mind. Mind exhibits this type of militancy when it takes its own ideas, whether moral or sensuous, for external realities, and this Santayana deems madness. The Sophists and the psychological empiricists were egotists, taking perceptions (sensuous fictions) for existences and denying the existence of anything they did not perceive. All concepts and categories, all assumptions, and all interpretations are to some extent arbitrary and therefore militant. Those which are public and shared are "normal," shaping perspectives of social interaction.[56] Militancy in the form of egotism is condemned by Santayana, but only in its more idiosyncratic forms. He reminds us that if mind were never militant, if we never believed our ideas were true, if we failed to formulate concepts (a kind of imposition of categories on nature), we could neither live nor think.

The German philosophers to whom Santayana first applied the name "egotist" were considered by him to be even more egotistical than the empiricists; rather than deny the existence of the world, they insisted that everything is mind's creation or the creation of equally subjective Will. Kant's categorical imperative, in giving the practical reason carte blanche to legislate for the universe, formulates the principle of *moral* militancy, the same as that which is embodied in any ideology. In politics it is found in the illusion of the "directive imagination." Like children, men believe that the utopias they dream up can be realized on earth just because they can imagine them. This belief presupposes the efficacy of thought, which Santayana denied in *The Life of Reason* and in the subsequent lively controversy with A. W. Moore.[57] His position on this score never changed, and in *Dominations and Powers* he charges that the idea that thought is efficacious is militant madness. "Directive imagination is not power: it is only that Nietzschean egotistical folly, the will to rule."[58] Circumstances sometimes permit our wishes to be fulfilled, but the imagination plays no part in bringing this about. Yet Santayana sees the directive imagination to be a dangerous symptom of underlying power which might, if successful, overwhelm the political system. Political parties, in *Dominations and Powers,* are portrayed as striving to rule in the interest of a special ideal. "A party in power is a blind engine, incapable of redirecting itself, and carried forward by the pledged and mortgaged imagination of all its members."[59] In their enthusiasm for its program, the members of a political party overlook many of the interests a government should serve, including private interests of their own, an omission they often discover too late. Santayana has ceased to believe that political parties can be rational or that political democracy, in a complex modern society, can be viable. He never explains in *Dominations and Powers* why a group cannot be motivated by the same rational discretion as an individual. He acknowledges the resentment of those who live under paternalistic rule but takes it to be misplaced, discounting the need for self-determination and for consciousness of freedom which, in other contexts, he takes to be so important.

Egotism in politics often takes the form of a people proclaiming itself the Chosen and usurping the right to dominate others. This, says Santayana, was the failing of the Jews, which they passed on to the Christians and the Moslems. The German people, too, on secular grounds, espoused the same militant end. "Unbelievers have a madness of their own: that theirs is the one race or the one philosophy predestined to rule the world, or to explain it."[60] This claim is said to be militant because a naturalist finds no evidence for predestination, which is therefore a disguised assertion of the Will to Power. Madmen do not see that history is not produced by dreams, or even by wisdom. The real explanation of the course of history lies, according to Santayana, in the realm of matter: "Transitions and catastrophes are not fruits of political calculation, but are forced on men by physical fatalities, as if by a change of weather."[61] Among the circumstances nature has imposed is the existing social and political order. We are caught in a web of conventions and customs and see the world in their light. But the secret truth is that our customary ways of doing things, our common understandings, our "normal madness," have evolved through ages of practical experience and met the tests life has imposed. To wish to change society is not simply heretical—Santayana finds no fault with heresy per se: "Those who break away from convention," he notes, "are usually right in thinking convention arbitrary and in some measure oppressive."[62] Utopian dreams may also be beautiful, and their source may be deep in human nature. But the lesson of Santayana's disillusioned politics is that human nature must bow to controlling circumstances and few dreams can come true. Furthermore, when a dream happens to be fulfilled, the fact of desire is only incidental to the eventuality, and for Santayana all plans seem to be dreams. If we were rational, as he conceives rationality, we would only desire what we are destined to get. But there would then be no great art, no religion, no scientific hypotheses, only a desert landscape of necessity from which, he tells us, we are fortunately and unwittingly saved, first, by the gratuitous attachment of spirit to the passionate interests of the psyche and, second, by the ability of spirit to transcend the actual in the contemplation of the formal and the desirable.

Describing the process of political upheaval, Santayana tries to show that apparently deliberate revolutionary changes are really inevitable and fatal, resting upon mutations in the political substructure. To see revolution in this light results in a particular moral judgment of it: some persons are bound to feel the imposition of any new regime to be a domination and a tyranny. But, says Santayana, if its time has not yet come, the tyranny will be overthrown; and if it endures, its tyrannical character (which is only an appearance, like all moral judgments) will fade since it is thus proved to be a natural growth taking root in soil which is prepared for it.[63] If we accept this materialist interpretation, there is no indeterminacy in the historical process and no real decision. The reasonable thing to do seems to be to understand events and yield gracefully to the inevitable. As Santayana himself puts it, "The world has caught us in a trap; but it did so when we were born, and we are used to the feeling."[64] But Santayana provides an escape. The life of the universe, as he presents it, is not a unitary process: many interests, many trends, many lives are all fighting for the same space, and resignation on the part of any one may spell defeat. It is necessary for some powers to prevail over others, and if we obey rational authority, we may succeed in directing events in a modest way after the fashion of economic art. By cultivating tendencies already implicit in the world, like the intelligent tyrant we may gain a degree of power, though this may have to be at the expense of other aims we have cherished.

When we recognize that even such economic rationality can arise only if and when mechanical forces produce it, we feel that Santayana has painted a grim picture, which seems still more forbidding because his view of tyranny does not appear to permit any ethical distinction between a tyrant and a moral representative. A moral representative is one who acts in the interest of those whom he would represent. But on Santayana's biological hypothesis, interests are impulses, and real interests are those which are adjusted to circumstances or which a creature nevertheless refuses to give up. They are, in short, those impulses which persist. A successful tyrant is a political agent riding the crest of a wave. He represents, whether he will or no, ascendant forces in society, which are by definition real interests. Though these may not be the only real interests, they are the only ones that are rational since they are the ones that are destined to be served. The only criterion for distinguishing a tyrant, it would seem, is ex post facto: if he is overthrown, it has been demonstrated that he does not speak for the powers at work in the country. If he remains in power and the state is remodelled after the pattern he proposes, the length of his tenure and the depth to which his power reaches are the measures of his representativeness.

Yet Santayana does caution that we must not "confuse the natural history of politics with rational government."[65] This was Machiavelli's error. It violates Santayana's doctrine of *ideal* realization to say that anything that comes to pass is therefore right. Rather than do so and surrender all ideals,

Santayana's naturalism allows us to consider the "real needs" of men and societies as providing norms according to which governments are to be judged. On the one view there can be no real tyranny; on the other, domination is actual, and we have a right to call it cruel. Santayana's own position is ambiguous, but the second of these views seems to be the key to the moral difference he sees between "the classic tradition" of governing men "according to a definite ideal system," which he respects, and what he calls autocratic idealism and construes to be the epitome of political militancy.[66] A modern state, he says, does not represent a people morally; its scope and authority are not determined by their interests, but by its control over territory. The constituent peoples are held in subjection in the service of an irrelevant political ideal, as in the shifting monarchies of Europe during the seventeenth and eighteenth centuries. In those *political* "nations," Santayana reflects, "there always remained a cleft and a maladaptation between the interests of the government and those of the various Peoples caught, by geographical and historical accidents, under its net." The result was a quick succession of revolutions, secessions, and temporary alliances, because "these landlord governments . . . did not represent the spontaneous generative order of society in all or perhaps in any of their provinces, but rather the domination of some military or doctrinal sect."[67] To govern thus, in the light of a purely political motive or doctrine, is *autocratically* militant. Despite his admiration for it, Santayana does not deny here that the classic tradition, too, contained elements of militancy and of autocracy as well; even "humane morals and traditional religions, if pressed," he asserts, "turn out to be sacrificial at bottom."[68] For whenever a maxim is adopted, the command implicit in it has been given precedence over future occurrences and represents an attempt to dictate to nature. However, Santayana views the classic tradition of the ancient Hebrews and Greeks as a habit of governing a people in the light of a moral ideal drawn from its own traditions and genius. Classical morality was closer to natural morality, spontaneous and "in sympathy with the procreative and poetic essence of animal and sensuous life," rather than critical of it.[69] The Hebrews were not directed by the Bible to realize a specific political ideal but were only to act in such a way that their God would make them prosperous. Unlike the Greeks of the Homeric age or the Hebrews of the Old Testament, Santayana sees political theorists such as Plato and Hegel to be truly autocratic idealists dedicated to fixed and artifical political conceptions.

To prescribe the interests of a people, or what is worse, to govern another people in one's own interest, is taken by Santayana to be autocratic, even when the ideal proposed is, like the classic tradition, expressive of the highest aspirations of its originators. He charges, on these grounds, that the Christians and Moslems were historically autocrats in their proselytizing zeal: "By disputation, zealous education, and on occasion by war, these religions were to be imposed and preserved in unchallenged domination."[70] So, too, he claims, "the two German wars and the sudden Russian threat of universal domination have proved that the classic tradition, passing through the German philosophy of history, drawn from the Bible, inspired the Russian Revolution and guides, most unexpectedly, a militant art of government intended to dominate the world."[71] And so too, he might add, any power, even a democracy, intent on installing in all the nations of the world its own form of rule and its own definition of "freedom" is no savior, but a militant dictator.

NOTES

[1] The parallelism with John Stuart Mill is unmistakable and is interesting in view of Santayana's opposition to the kind of liberalism Mill represents. Cf. *On Liberty,* Chapter I.

[2] *DP,* p. 65.

[3] Cf. *ibid.,* pp. 60–70.

[4] *RCS,* p. 21; cf. Sterling Lamprecht, "Normal Madness and the Political Life," *The Journal of Philosophy,* XLIX, No. 7 (March 27, 1952), 208–14.

[5] *Philosophical Review,* LXI, No. 3 (July, 1952), 400–407; cf. p. 401.

[6] *DP,* p. 126; cf. also *EGP,* pp. 108–22.

[7] *EGP,* p. 121.

[8] *DP,* p. 177.

[9] Cf. *ibid.,* p. 430.

[10] *Ibid.,* p. 23.

[11] Cf. *ibid.,* pp. 303–7; also *SE,* pp. 128–39.

[12] *DP,* p. 305.

[13] *Ibid.,* p. 295.

[14] *Ibid.,* p. 460.

[15] Cf. Sterling Lamprecht, *op. cit.*

[16] *DP,* pp. 177–78.

[17] *Ibid.,* p. 178.

[18] *Ibid.,* p. 179.

[19] *Ibid.*

[20] *Ibid.,* p. 41. The inconsistency in Santayana's use of the term "Will" is discussed below and again in Chapter VIII.

[21] *Ibid.,* note.

[22] *Ibid.,* p. 295.

[23] *Ibid.,* p. 26.

[24] *Ibid.,* p. 177.

[25] *Ibid.,* p. 91.

[26] *Ibid.,* p. 363.

[27] *Ibid.,* p. 200.

[28] *Ibid.,* p. 199.

[29] *Ibid.,* p. 201.

[30] *Ibid.,* p. 163.

[31] *Ibid.,* pp. 430–31.

[32] Socrates, in the first of Santayana's two dialogues "On Self-Government," *DL,* p. 105.

[33] *DP,* p. 378.

[34] *Ibid.,* p. 422.

[35] *Ibid.,* p. 226.

[36] *Ibid.,* p. 364.

[37] *Ibid.,* p. 363.

[38] George H. Sabine, *op. cit.,* p. 403.

[39] *DP,* p. ix.

[40] *Ibid.,* p. 221.

[41] *Ibid.,* p. 210.

[42] *Ibid.*

[43] *GTB,* pp. 7–8.

[44] Cf. *DP,* p. 210.

[45] George H. Sabine, *op. cit.,* p. 405.

[46] *DP,* p. 433.

[47] *Ibid.,* p. 325.

[48] "A political philosophy which turns upon the contrast between the natural and the artificial depends less upon any definite meaning that attaches to the word 'nature' than upon the selection of an appropriate analogy for judging the deficiencies of the state of affairs it criticizes. In the long history of this kind of theory two analogies have mainly prevailed, that of the contract, in theories which were directed against an authority felt to be oppressive, and that of the family, in theories which sought to re-establish authority in a situation felt to be anarchic. Mr. Santayana's political theory is explicitly of the latter type. . . ." George H. Sabine, *op. cit.,* p. 404.

[49] *DP.,* p. 109.

[50] *DP.,* pp. 208–12; pp. 271–75.

[51] *DP,* p. 431.

[52] *Ibid.,* p. 210.

[53] Cf. *GTB,* pp. 72–73.

[54] *EGP,* p. 6.

[55] *DP*, p. 328.

[56] Cf. Democritus' thesis in "Normal Madness," *DL*, pp. 36–57.

[57] Cf. "The Efficacy of Thought," *The Journal of Philosophy, Psychology, and Scientific Methods*, III, No. 15 (July 19, 1906), 410–12.

[58] *DP*, p. 124.

[59] *Ibid.*, p. 125.

[60] *Ibid.*, p. 234.

[61] *Ibid.*, p. 221.

[62] *Ibid.*, p. 222.

[63] Cf. *ibid.*, pp. 220–23.

[64] *Ibid.*, pp. 221–22.

[65] *Ibid.*, p. 209.

[66] *Ibid.*, pp. 272–73.

[67] *Ibid.*, p. 391.

[68] *Ibid.*, p. 392.

[69] *Ibid.*

[70] *Ibid.*, p. 273.

[71] *Ibid.*, p. 274.

CHAPTER 8

The Moral Economy

THE TERM "RATIONALITY" is one of those which Santayana uses in a number of subtly different, though related, senses. In *Dominations and Powers* it has special connotations expressive of the author's disillusion. Santayana has not lost faith in reason, but he has adopted a different and more modest conception of its nature, function, and implications, a conception which seems to be a stricter articulation of his thesis that thought is a reflection of, and not a directive factor in, action. In all of his writings Santayana takes rationality in any sense to be, like morality, introduced into the world by mind. He consistently takes *intelligibility* to be an interpretation of existing reality, not one of its properties. And he suggests, in *Dominations and Powers,* that language, first, and then mathematics and science "superpose" a network of relations upon experience. These relations reflect (perhaps "repeat" would be more accurate) regularities occurring among ideas present in awareness. When "rational description" is applied to *existence,* it is by "imaginative presumption." The relations reason perceives between essences present to intuition do prove relevant to experience, indicating, Santayana says, that we are justified in inferring regularities in the natural flux; but he describes the practical application of reason, nevertheless, as being in actuality a kind of "shrewd divination" and "purely speculative."[1]

Rational interpretation is especially risky in the spheres of human history and politics where, Santayana holds, the things we study are so large and so complex, and our perceptions so fragmented and peripheral, that art must provide form and continuity. But in a second sense, the concept of rationality *is* applicable to history, society, and politics, although it stands for an ideal which is only partially realizable. *Moral rationality,* such as that achieved spontaneously in parenthood, is a harmony of impulses or interests. In a complex society interests are divergent, and if they are not somehow modified, conflict is inevitable. Ideally, Santayana suggests, even in *Dominations and Powers,* they can be harmonized by wise government.

A third sense of rationality, which constitutes its root meaning in Santayana's political philosophy, is *adjustment.* "The life of reason" can be charac-

101

terized as that life in which impulses are mutually adjusted and reconciled with the natural agencies that surround and support them. The ideational dimension of the rational life is consequent upon the harmony thus attained. Rational action, the method of intelligence, is shown in Santayana's early works to combine the dialectical articulation of intent with "docility," plasticity, the ability to conform to the requirements of external necessity. The same duality is emphasized in the concept of rational authority in *Dominations and Powers*. Rational authority is carefully defined as a relation between primal impulse, or Will, and environing circumstances, but while both Will and circumstances are authoritative, the burden of rendering a policy "rational" rests with the latter. This doctrine has important ramifications in Santayana's political philosophy. Policy originates in impulse, and the primal and irrefutable justification of impulse is simply that it occurs; but in itself impulse is neither rational nor irrational. Santayana judges its rationality in the light of its possible consummation. His theory is that primal Will, the driving force in action, is blind to the value of that action, but when frustrated, Will gives rise to a criterion of rationality: "That which makes an action rational is the material possibility of carrying it out successfully. In a word, *Circumstances* render one action rational and another irrational."[2] This is Santayana's proposed criterion of rationality in conduct and in government, and the standard according to which political movements and social reforms are to be evaluated: not only must a given policy actually reflect the real needs of a people, but in order to be rational it must be viable. It must be "not only demanded by the present, but organically *acceptable for the future*."[3]

In *Dominations and Powers* Santayana takes the rational in this sense to be one with the right. "When," he asks, "has a political movement or institution rational authority? When is it 'right'?" Right and wrong, according to Santayana, are always relative to need, on the one hand, and circumstances, on the other. There are no absolute or intrinsic values, and, taken abstractly, moral judgments are irrelevant and unjustifiably dogmatic. Rationality and rightness are said by him to be intrinsically relative, "for it is their relativity that makes them relevant to events in the world. Were they absolute, and irrelevant to human nature and circumstances, they would be pathological fixations, making for militant madness."[4] Once given the primal, impulsive Will, it would seem, nature in effect proclaims those policies "right" which it permits to be carried out successfully, and those institutions "rational" which it supports. This is the principle which dominates Santayana's most pessimistic passages. The most optimistic statement of it would construe rationality to consist in sensitive adaptation. Circumstances may be rendered more favorable by active intervention, but to the extent that action succeeds in modifying circumstances in the first place, Santayana observes, it is already well adapted, and hence it is already rational.

The proposition that the right is what serves an interested party seems to contradict the assertion that the right is what is possible. Santayana combines the two, judiciously concluding that the impossible cannot be good, that to idealize perfect happiness or absolute good is good religion but bad politics, and that to fight for the unattainable on earth is militant ignorance. His position is not, however, perfectly clear-cut: at several points he tries to reconcile a moral relativism which defines good and right in terms of *need* with a political application of naturalism which takes *power* to be right and rationality to consist in the acceptance of necessity. Santayana's moral naturalism, derived from the humane ethics of the Greeks and Spinoza, is occasionally transmuted, in its political application, into a view which combines a version of Social Darwinism and the thesis that power is right. In his political writings he moves between the charitable position that no one thing is, in itself, more right than any other and that of *Realpolitik,* according to which whatever is, is right.

Adopting the latter thesis may lead to the elevation of the survival of the fittest to the status of a moral principle. This tendency to Social Darwinism characterized Santayana from the start. In a passage in *Reason in Society,* for instance, the value of a political system is measured in terms of its strength:

. . . those types of polity which . . . go with strength, presumably represent the better adjustment to natural conditions, and therefore the better ideal. Though the substance of ideals is the will, their mould must be experience and a true discernment of opportunity; so that while all ideals, regarded *in vacuo,* are equal in ideality, they are, under given circumstances, very diverse in worth.[5]

One might take Santayana to be saying *only* that power is a sign or mark of rationality—which he does indeed hold—but in the passage cited he is developing the thesis that conquest, in giving scope to a stronger and better-adapted nation, is a vehicle of progress. Note that the general principle implicit in this assertion equates strength with virtue. If the stronger and more successful is the better, does it not follow that any order which supplants another is therefore superior? If so, social change is necessarily progress, a conclusion we know Santayana rejects. Progress, as he defines it, is relative, defined by consciousness of an end toward which behavior is directed. I believe that this particular contradiction is evidence of a fundamental inconsistency in Santayana's politics.

The analysis of tyranny in *Dominations and Powers* also illustrates the thesis that the successful is the rational and therefore is right: if a tyranny becomes established and legally sanctioned and the public ceases to object to it, "it ceases to be a tyranny and becomes a normal constitutional government."[6] Now, if a successful tyranny is to be given rational approval on the grounds of its actual imposition, do we not have to ask whether the other principle of rational authority, the authority of primal Will or psyche, has been violated? If a better ideal has been substituted for a worse one, it would seem that the interest of the conquered people has been served. But better and worse, on the assumption of Santayana's interest theory of value, are to be decided only in relation to the actual needs of the individual for whom the thing to be assessed has value. Perhaps no one should be truly said to need anything if it is unattainable, but this is not equivalent to, nor would Santayana accept, the proposition that everything that is attained is good. A regime which does not serve the interest of the governed is, by his own definition, a domination and, from the point of view of those affected by it, is evil.

One of the problems of moral relativism is, of course, how we are to define "interest." Santayana equates interest with need rather than with wish or desire. Need, on his biological hypothesis, is rooted in impulse, in the actual tendencies of an organism, its vital Will or psyche. Santayana's concept is clearly derived from Spinoza's *"conatus."* "Psyche" is defined, in *The Realm of Spirit,* as "a particular instance of universal Will," of *"the observable endeavor in things of any sort to develop a specific form and to preserve it."*[7] This endeavor is the substance of need. Schopenhauer's concept of Will, which Santayana also explicitly adopts, is a similar interpretation of the general dynamism of nature. But here, as in other places, Santayana is not consistent. "Will," for him, means alternately (1) "mechanical momentum," or "vital inertia," and (2) the very different motivation of an animal, the "eager" activity which Santayana refers to as a modification of the mechanical life of nature.[8] This ambiguity does not affect Santayana's basic thesis that value is a function of impulse and that morality and politics arise and exist only in the relations between psyches and circumstances. While, for him, life is not a good in itself, the Will of a living organism is the sole source of value. Good and evil only arise when a psyche encounters something which either serves it instrumentally and as a source of satisfaction or impedes its progress.

Psyche is responsive as well as active, but, according to this view, its responsiveness is an expression of its impulsive direction. Needs may not always be felt or cognized, but, for Santayana, there can be no need which is not the expression of some movement on the part of or within an organism. It is worth noting that such a biological interpretation of "need" would seem to disallow needs which are defined, not by the presence of any tendency, but by its absence. A consequence of this assumption, as will be shown, is that Santayana would consider it wrong to *create* needs in a person or a society. Santayana specifies that the criterion for the true good of an individual or a society is *internal* to it, in its native impulses and habitual tendencies. If anyone, he says, pretended to govern in the name of the Will of a monarch, or that of God or nature, let alone in the interest of a foreign nation, "the power exercised by that government would be an instance of militant domination."[9] This contention seems to be directly contrary to the thesis that a successful imposition is to be considered rational, and one wonders how the two can be reconciled. A possible interpretation of Santayana's position is that whereas from the point of view of one form of life another might be a domination, in a disinterested and rational perspective both are equally natural, and neither is better in itself. Strictly, they are incomparable, and the fact of domination has no intrinsic moral quality. Santayana would also claim that no one, no people, has a *right* to the satisfaction of its needs, and that, in the end, the mechanical forces which give rise to all ideals determine which deserve to survive and which to perish.

No government, according to Santayana, and no form of government, is intrinsically rational or disinterested. It may function disinterestedly in its *method,* but in working for (just as in working against) the good of a particular people, any government is militant. "Other men or other interests than those a government serves form, from its point of view, a part of the world of things" or of circumstances.[10] *Rational* government would minimize the conflict of Wills within its domain, and mediate between them and their environment. But Santayana would take its commitment to those Wills to be arbitrary, even if he would call it rational because it is morally representative. No commitment is per se rational, on this view, but only natural; commitment is the ground of morality but is never either right or wrong in itself. Thus, Santayana would find no *rational* justification for condemning a specific domination.

The conquest Santayana praises would seem to be the conquest of a people he deems morally weak by a nation whose civilization he values more highly. For example, he says in *Reason in Society,* "What the Orient owes to Greece, the Occident to Rome, India to England, native America to Spain, is a civilisation incomparably better than that which the conquered people could ever have provided for themselves."[11] In principle, a powerful nation will prevail. It might be pointed out that in practice, domination of a people with a definite and virile "genius," as Santayana puts it, might be economically or militarily successful, but it would be a moral failure, its defeat expressing the final judgment of nature. A morally weak nation will very likely be conquered in the end, even if it is militarily powerful; if what Santayana calls the Will of the subject people is coherent enough, the domination will not succeed in the long run. This is, in point of fact, what happened to the successive conquerors of China, whose cultures were absorbed and modified by the conquered people. Thus *moral* conquest is an index of the strength and coherence of those impulses which Santayana takes to underlie civilization. If they are weak, he would find nothing worth preserving; and to try to prop up a morally weak nation, he would very likely say, is only to postpone the sentence which nature will inevitably pronounce.

Like rational ethics, for Santayana politics, the study of political right and wrong, is properly grounded in factual, physical science. According to his moral relativism, all norms are to be derived from actual biological drives and are necessarily so derived, since, for a naturalist, the formulation of even a supernatural or abstract ideal is the work of a biological individual. But not all ideals are representative of basic needs; some are ephemeral, and Santayana judges the effort to make these prevail to be irrationally militant and counter to more fundamental tendencies. The principle of need, as it might be called, implies that only widespread and enduring social goals, whether or not they are consciously entertained, are potentially rational. To be legitimate, Santayana says, legislation must represent "massive generative movements and not thinly militant strains" or factional eruptions.[12] His definition of a rational political program, then, conceives of it as one that would carry out as far as possible the spontaneous and generic impulses of the governed. To the extent that they can be sustained, Santayana would say, these comprise their true "interest." According to this interpretation, rational government would promote the "natural" development of incipient tendencies rather than autocratically redirect movement and growth in the interest of ideals considered more worthy than those which a society has evolved itself. To be rational, a government must promote the interest of the governed since to do so is part of the meaning of rational authority: the principle of moral representation, of obedience to the authority of the Will. It is clear that if interest is defined solely by existing tendencies, actual domination should always be judged irrational. Again, on this assumption it would never be rational for a ruler to institute fundamental social changes. The principle of need would not permit the substitution of an ideal which is foreign to a people for one which is native. For example, it would not seem to be rational, by Santayana's definition, to "assist" an agrarian people to transform its economy into an industrial system in the absence of an indigenous movement in that direction. But the principle of natural authority would appear to make a *successful* imposition a rational one. And the doctrine of the authority of primal Will is not the thesis that a people has a *right* to its ideals. To claim any rights a priori Santayana would consider ethical absolutism, to which he opposes a relativism which admires what anyone finds beautiful or precious but neither expects it to survive nor fights for its survival, nor even condemns the forces that destroy it, for they have their own beauty and their own value. It is my opinion that Santayana never resolves the contradictions within his theory of value. His respect for coherence and strength enables him to accept conquest as a fact of life and even to admire it, while his commitment to ideals prevents him from wholeheartedly accepting the Nietzschean condemnation of ideals which are doomed to defeat as, in the end, are all ends and all values.

On Santayana's materialist interpretation of politics, there is no such thing as "natural right" in the sense of universal or imprescriptible personal or political rights. Not liberty, nor even life itself, is a right for anyone, but only a natural ideal. The Will, by nature, resists limitation and restriction, and therefore each of us feels liberty to be his right; "yet in the economy of nature," Santayana asserts, "there is no such thing as a right. Existence itself is an unearned gift and an imposed predicament."[13] In the generative order of society there are only organisms. Each individual has a Will and commands a degree of power, but the assertion of a right is a moral claim, and unless it is somehow justified, Santayana holds such a claim to be a fictional and egotistical projection upon reality of one's own desires. For Santayana, as for Spinoza, whom he admired and whose moral naturalism and relativism he believed himself to have adopted, nature is, *simpliciter:* its moral qualities only arise for individuals under particular conditions. That anything is right or wrong, that anyone has a specific right would, according to this view, have to be equally partial interpretations reflecting the bias of an interested party. As Spinoza conceived it, according to Santayana, "the infinite knows no obligation, it is subject to no standard."[14]

Yet Spinoza and Santayana each accept a version of the doctrine of natural right, which locates the source of the moral within the natural. In the *Political Treatise* Spinoza states that "every natural thing has by nature as much right as it has power to exist and operate."[15] Santayana's analogous suggestion is that "you have a right to be what you are and to become what you become."[16] The justification of Spinoza's principle is in his monistic conception of Substance and the notion of the identity of the power and the right of God. Santayana's doctrine is grounded in his materialism, and specifically in the concept of a pluralistic universe in which no moral perspective has priority over any other. For Spinoza, the right of an individual is logically necessary and consequent upon his nature; the individual's powers are but instances of the powers of Nature, illustrations of the laws which express the being of God. Santayana similarly bases right on nature, not on any logical necessity in existence, but on the relation between the powers of the individual and the natural circumstances in which he operates. In adapting to natural conditions an individual or a group wins the power, and hence the right, to live and to be free. This is what Santayana claims to mean by his thesis that "Might is Right," where right is held to be rationally justified since it is conferred by natural authority.[17]

Successful adjustment is, for Santayana, freedom, or what he calls *vital liberty*. As a materialist, he rejects the hypothesis of an uncaused will; on the same grounds he denies that action is rationally determined, holding that choices are acts of physical organisms and therefore mechanically caused. The psyche, the "hidden self" which Santayana makes the source of action, is, "like every other centre or kind of movement in nature, perfectly contingent in being groundlessly determinate," having no logical justification and being subject to no logical necessity.[18] Being part of nature, the biological self is, therefore, logically free, but freedom of this sort is trivial. The first freedom Santayana considers morally significant is the exercise of natural powers in harmony with circumstances, the cooperation of impulse and environment. Liberty must consist in such cooperation; since rebellion against nature results in frustration, militant idealism condemns us to slavery.

That which the world allows and encourages may be the opposite of that which we truly prize, believe, and are competent to do: so that experience, instead of tending to create a harmony between vital liberty and lifelong practice, perhaps closes all the hatches down upon that liberty and condemns the true soul to voyage blind and captive below deck, while pirate circumstances sail the vessel.[19]

This is the predicament in which Santayana finds the moral animal. He is only free when he has relinquished the freedom to resist overwhelming power, since in rebelling he loses the possibility of controlling his own fate. The only escape Santayana sees for him is into the realm of the ideal which, though it may be irresistible and yield its own satisfactions, practically is valueless.

When an organism with a highly developed nervous system achieves a vital harmony, Santayana suggests, it becomes conscious. Spirit, awakening in it, lends the fortunate creature a new dimension of freedom which it would not otherwise attain, for in entertaining ideas spirit escapes the necessity of action and the pain of frustration. Santayana calls this moral transcendence *spiritual freedom*. Both concepts, vital liberty and spiritual freedom, enter into his notion of a *rational order of society;* the criterion of rationality in the social order is the provision of freedom.

Under the heading "The Rational Order of Society," in *Dominations and Powers,* Santayana considers three different, though interrelated, things. The first is the whole system of powers and dominations which constitutes a society, viewed as what I suggest be called a "moral economy." This dimension of society is called the rational order because it is *potentially* rational. In a second, honorific sense, a rational order of society resembles, though it differs in significant respects from, a societal ideal of the traditional sort. Santayana once called it an "imaginary" order.[20] The ideal social order of *Dominations and Powers* is not a fixed political or economic system, but a model of rationality in the moral economy, characterized by its metaphorical name, "Many Nations in One Empire."[21] Thirdly, Santayana applies the concept of rational order to the method of rational government.

In its first and broadest signification the rational order of society is society itself, viewed in the light of "some ideal of the free uses to be made of life, when food has been secured, tolerable in quantity and quality."[22] It is therefore said to be an "economic order." In introducing his major categories, Santayana defines this order of society in terms of the relative proportion of "necessary and optional arts." But in "Book Third," devoted to the rational order of society, the concept of a specifically economic order is generalized, and, when fully articulated, the term signifies *the balance of control and freedom, of order and liberty, in a social system.* The rational order of society is, therefore, more aptly characterized as a moral than as an economic order. If we take the word "economy" to denote the management of a system, we are justified in calling this a moral economy. Santayana himself employs the expression "moral economy," but, for the most part, only loosely. I propose to use it as the name for what I consider to be the main category in the description of the rational order of society. Like many of Santayana's terms, the term "moral economy" does not always have the same referent, nor is it fully defined in connection with any single occurrence. It must be understood as it is contextually defined wherever it or its equivalents appear. Nevertheless, it is possible to discover in *Dominations and Powers* a systematic portrayal of society as a moral economy, having two major aspects, one economic in the narrower sense, the other political.

"The interplay of economic and liberal arts" is a moral economy, i.e., an arrangement of functions which may promote or inhibit freedom. "Liberal" arts are distinguished from "mechanical or industrial" arts in *Reason in Art.* Industrial art is instrumental, the "servile" process of turning nature to human uses. The liberal stage of art, art in its "nobler" sense, is a spontaneous, inherently satisfying, and "self-justifying" activity. Santayana considers liberal art to be "perfection in action," as the contemplation of essences is perfection in thought.[23] The term "perfection," in Santayana's writings, sometimes means simply harmonious and unimpeded functioning; it also refers to the final stage of a development or the complete embodiment of any form. Perfection in both senses may be implied by the term "ideal," which also connotes "immaterial" and sometimes specifically "mental." In liberal art, he writes, "perfectly fit matter is appropriated to ideal uses and endowed with a direct spiritual function."[24] That is, a suitable medium is at hand and is, for no ulterior purpose, given a form which is felt to be both harmonious and eloquent, expressing and clarifying (i.e., formulating) the conception which accompanies (though it does not direct) its creation. The work of art is thus ideal in its status as an expression of the harmony of the powers that produced it, as well as in the perfection of its form and in its contemplative essence. Liberal art, to Santayana, is an exercise in moral idealism and the paradigm of the life of reason. Conversely, the life of reason is the life in which art "subserves all parts of the human ideal."[25]

The same conception of liberal art is developed in *Dominations and Powers,* where it is no longer integral to the concept of the life of reason, but plays an important part in the definition of a rational society. Since he does not have to struggle against the limitations of matter but exploits its potentialities, the artist is free in the sense intended by the term "vital liberty." And in conceiving the forms he gives to his work, the artist is also free in the sense of "spiritual freedom." In the later book liberal art is likened to play. A liberal art is "a free, happy, and enlightening occupation, its own reward."[26] Any art is liberal when pursued for its own sake, and even mundane occupations, when they become rhythmic and pleasurable, Santayana believes to have a liberal dimension. When an art is liberal, he says, its products will be good, not for their use, but for their "beauty," their service to the spirit. In their contemplation spirit "finds the vital echo of its potential experiences in their emotional urgency and colour, without the irrecoverable and distracting detail of their accidental occasions."[27] The dimension of moral idealism is not absent: according to Santayana works of art are meaningful because they express truths of human experience. Playing in a medium, with no ulterior end, an artist insinuates into matter forms to which he responds emotionally because they are symbolic of his ideals. It is the free play of the imagination in the enjoyment of *ideals* thus personified which Santayana identifies most closely with happiness. In facilitating this "spiritual self-transcendence," liberal art is participation in what he calls the spiritual life, when he uses that expression to refer, not to the sheer contemplation of essences, but to a vision of goods and beauties. That this is an important, if not the dominant, meaning of "spirituality" for him is revealed in *Platonism and the Spiritual Life:*

. . . perfect impartiality is not human; it is contrary to the initial status of spirit, as the hypostatic synthetic expression and realization of some discursive phase of animal life—some adventure, some predicament, some propensity, some preoccupation. It is therefore natural that the intrinsic infinity of Being should remain in the background even in the spiritual life, and that essences should be contemplated and distinguished rather as ideals for the human imagination than as beings necessary in themselves.[28]

In *Dominations and Powers,* for example, religion is said to be liberal when it expresses in a dramatic and compelling form, as in the Gospels, "moral truth or familiar human predicaments," which we can view in their moral and emotional significance for us.[29] When it is political, on the other hand, religion (like government) is an economic art. In the same way, when it is used "symbolically," as in poetry, language has a liberal function, in contrast to its use for practical or economic ends.

In *Dominations and Powers* all art and all industry are said to have originated in free play. "Life itself is play."[30] Santayana takes the liberal dimension of human activity to be primal and generic, so that it provides him with a norm according to which, as a naturalist, he may formulate moral and political standards. Freedom, he discovers, is universally sought, even though absolute freedom, "vacant freedom," is unattainable (since to exist is to be specific and hence limited), and liberty must always take different shapes.[31] In Protestant societies play is usually condemned as unnecessary diversion, if not actual sin. Not only does Santayana make free play the end and aim of life, it is also the first ingredient in work itself. All animal activity, he says, is spontaneous and free; freedom is limited only by the press of psyches competing with one another and by the impact of environmental forces. The generative order of society is embodied in primal Will, which always and everywhere seeks opportunities for expression. Even when the ascendance of one power results in the death of another, it is a victory for vital liberty since life of one sort is not less vital than any other. "Only external material cataclysms or failure of supplies could kill the generative power that, pressed and compressed as it may be by circumstances, is pressed and compressed only because it is spontaneously intent on play."[32] But if life were all play, it would be self-defeating, for it is only by means of instrumental arts that animals can overcome the natural obstacles to self-realization. The problem Santayana assigns to the moral economist is to discover a satisfactory balance between work and play, to channel human activities in such a way that the economy provides the widest scope for spirit without endangering the social order.

The fundamental difference between economic and liberal art, according to Santayana, is that in so far as it is liberal, action is both spontaneous and nicely adjusted. "Your compulsions have become your choices and your limitations your virtues."[33] This is the essence of vital liberty. In contrast, economic art, consisting in overcoming barriers to free play, is essentially militant. But industry creates the opportunity for spontaneous flights, so that even in the "fine arts," art is always an interplay of economic and liberal activity, and freedom always the product of order and limitation. A rational life is now seen by Santayana to be art in this inclusive sense. "The complete art of living," he says in *Dominations and Powers*, "would be economic in its arts for the sake of being wholly liberal in its enjoyments."[34] *A rational society*, on the same grounds, would be one which would establish the necessary conditions for the widest possible achievement of the ideal of liberal art, action spontaneously adjusted to its conditions and therefore free. In such a rational society life could be lived for its own sake, Santayana tells us, and be enjoyable in its own right, not "servile" as it is in industrial societies, where man himself is first among the raw materials of industry and is enslaved by the civilization he has created.

One aspect of liberal art, as Santayana describes it, is the vital liberty realized in the creative process. The other is the spiritual freedom to which it gives rise, the escape it provides "into the freedom of ideal creations, as from the stress of earthly passions under the spell of music."[35] Because it is the setting for the realization of spiritual freedom, the economic order of arts, which is one facet of the moral economy, may also be called "the spiritual economy."

The second and politically more important aspect of the moral economy is the relation between society and government. In this relation vital liberty will be attained when government furthers the real interest of the governed. We may call this phase of social interaction the political order, not because government is political, but because the freedom which government can insure is the freedom of moral agents to determine their own policies. This freedom may be called political, but Santayana occasionally refers to it as *moral freedom*, a term which avoids the narrow associations of the word "politics." Like the expression "the moral economy," "moral freedom" is not used by Santayana as the official title of a category, but it aptly describes a concept which is central to his systematic social and political thought, and it occurs both in *The Life of Reason* and *Dominations and Powers*. Moral freedom, in the later book, is a necessary condition of vital liberty. If vital liberty is spontaneous and adjusted action, free from distraction, moral freedom is the absence of external domination which would frustrate, divert, or impede that action. Vital liberty might be said to be self-realization. Moral freedom is self-determination; it is the freedom to adhere to ideals which grow out of one's own character.[36] Moral freedom is "liberty to pursue some possible good towards which that psyche is already directed, and to which it presupposes itself to remain attached."[37] This implies both the absence of external coercion and the rejection of momentary impulses or militant and unrealizable aims.

The full meaning of moral freedom rests on Santayana's conviction that liberty, rather than being antithetical to discipline, depends on the latter; we might say that for him liberty consists in discipline.[38] While the response to a specific domination is often a struggle on the part of the psyche for complete independence from any sort of limitations, Santayana insists that this "vacant freedom" is an ontological impossibility and a moral contradiction. To exist is to be individual, to be determinate, and therefore to have potentialities for specific "ideal realizations" to the exclusion of others. To try to escape all limitation is futile, since such escape would be the cessation of existence. Freedom from one set of limitations can only take the form of submission to another.

Moral freedom is the freedom to pursue ends expressive of one's own nature and experience. But the development of the self is the acquisition of distinction, the progressive narrowing of possible avenues of self-realization, and the limitation of vacant freedom. This has the corollary of concentrating vital energies, of producing that sort of "harmony in strength" which Santayana associates with moral excellence. The prerequisite of vital liberty, as he sees it, is not indeterminacy or abandon but *integrity*: coherence and freedom from distraction on the part of the psyche. Because even within a single individual, nature is diverse and impulses conflict, Santayana maintains that liberty presupposes government. In the first place, he holds that any organism may have only a "mock freedom" since it is only possible for it to exert itself in certain ways; it cannot choose to act in ways beyond its capacity, nor is it free not to act at all. But secondly, the *sense* of freedom arises when the organism is so perfectly adjusted that it automatically conforms to circumstances. Therefore, Santayana says, "in order to live without control and absolutely ungoverned, as the spirit thinks it lives, it must be controlled by an organism that governs itself. In other words, it cannot be anarchical, but must be inwardly, precisely, and irretrievably governed."[39] Vital liberty, then, is not uninhibited primal spontaneity or anarchic self-indulgence. In a sense freedom is a delusion, for it is really a high discipline.

For Santayana, integrity and inner coherence are not sufficient conditions of freedom, which also presupposes adjustment to the environment. "The substance and joy of liberty begin only when the well-integrated powers of the psyche find or establish a world in which they bear their specific and appropriate fruit."[40] That it is possible to try to make the world a more comfortable home for the psyche is stated clearly enough, but Santayana more often emphasizes adjustment *to* circumstances than adjustment *of* them. Even intelligence, by his definition, is not a matter of deliberately altering conditions but of adapting to them so well that a purposive conception which arises at the beginning of an act is actually predictive of its end. This doctrine is perhaps the most striking consequence of epiphenomenalism and has the greatest import for Santayana's conception of rationality.

This is the greatest feat, as far as we know, that the generative order of nature has ever accomplished. The teleology visible in all self-repeating processes, where the beginning of each phase or beat is pregnant with the end, here becomes rational art; for here a living being produces a result that it had actually preconceived and desired. Sensibility, intrinsically merely an aesthetic overflow of organic life, now has acquired the moral dignity of intellectual and emotional accommodation with nature or with the "Will of God."[41]

Freedom, for Santayana, if we are talking of what he called "vital liberty," is just this accommodation. To speak of freedom in any absolute or untrammeled sense would be nonsense: we might momentarily *feel* free, he says, but the feeling is not actual freedom. Spiritual freedom, "domination (i.e., understanding) of existence by consciousness, forgetting practical involvement in it, is conceived to presuppose this adjustment. Rather than influence or control over nature, Santayana's concept of spiritual freedom implies acceptance of the adjustment upon which spirit or mind is dependent and comprehension of the situation in which psyche finds itself. The *inner* liberty of spirit is "the very vitality of its body and of its world here now actualized and become conscious."[42] Spirit is still "captive," its vision structured by the confluence of powers in the organism, but it expresses the coherence and the settled character of its source.

The essence of spiritual freedom, Santayana says, is the "impartiality" which comes of understanding, the detachment produced by knowledge of "how things actually grow and work."[43] In becoming conscious, intelligence perceives essences which, when psyche is well adjusted, are dependable indicators of the course of nature. In entertaining these essences and the relations among them, spirit transcends the limits of "every vital and moral perspective," its insights becoming "hypothetical and ideal" as in mathematics or science. The philosophic mind, developing this self-transcendence, cultivates a broader perspective and a longer view. In studying its surroundings, such a mind "will discover that the order of society is unstable, and in the very act of studying the various forms of order and comparing their fruits, it will absolve itself from blind allegiance to any one of them."[44] Santayana accepts the fact that perfect impartiality is impossible for spirit arising in an individual life, for the perspective of any moral center determines its vision; but charity may be enlarged, and, he believes, we may learn to view existence in all its forms, including the forms of society, "under the aspect of eternity." In this way we arrive at a "rational" political ideal.

For a creature that lives in society, Santayana understands that vital liberty and moral freedom cannot be described in terms of an individual life alone; the social conditions which contribute to his character and condition his freedom must also be accounted for. As Santayana sees society, it is composed of diverse groups such as ethnic and religious bodies, each of which may be said to compose a society, as he defines it, and to which he applies the term "moral society."[45] The integrity of an individual is, in part, a social product, while the integrity of a society is visible in its members. The concept of a moral society is central to the definition of the rational order of society in the second, ideal sense.

Whereas a society, not being an organism, is not said to have a Will, Santayana holds that its institutions channel individual energies, determining the society's identity and defining its ideals. As delineated in *Dominations and Powers,* a society is an association or cooperation of individual agents, of psyches or Wills. It is, therefore, a modification of the generative order of nature: "Society exists by a conspiracy of physiological forces."[46] These forces are the ultimate source of the meanings and values to be fostered by government. The powers which form society are embodied in individuals, each of whom Santayana says is moved by "inward invisible specific springs of action called instincts, needs, passions, or interests."[47] Since he considers motivation to be physical, unconscious, efficient causation, and internal to the organism, Santayana views society as a secondary order, "a unit only for apprehension, covering a variable and diffused concourse of separate lives and interests."[48] But as a system of dynamic organisms and as a product of their history, a society is a form of life; hence Santayana views it as a source of authority and the legitimate object of both political interest and free identification. The traditional organization of society is presented in *Dominations and Powers* as a natural authority, analogous to the individual psyche with its distinctive personal characteristics. If government is to be rational, it must be morally representative, representative of the generative order of society. That is, it must mediate between social organizations and their environment.

Despite his biological and atomistic conception of mental and moral life, Santayana, from the very first, laid great stress on the social dimension of ideals. In this connection I disagree with Vivas, who asserts that Santayana, in writing *The Life of Reason,* seems unaware that ideals grow out of a social, as well as a biological, ground.[49] Patriotism, for instance, could not arise as a purely individual ideal; but even in areas where individual activity has greatest weight, Santayana makes it quite clear that he thinks there could be no great individual ideals, no individual excellence, and no high achievements in the absence of the traditional symbols and inherited values of civilization. This is explicitly stated in both *Reason in Society* and *Reason in Science* and is the heart of Santayana's doctrine of race.[50] Santayana places society, with its totems and taboos, at the core of moral and spiritual life. Commenting on Santayana's naturalistic approach to morality, Munitz remarks that, for Santayana, "morality, the principle of all choices in taste, faith, and allegiance has its natural basis in an inherited animal and social structure."[51] Beyond this, in *The Life of Reason* and also in *Dominations and Powers*, Santayana conceives the potential scope of personal interest to include the whole network of societies to which an individual belongs, and sees personal liberty, both moral and spiritual, to be in large measure a function of social order.

In *Dominations and Powers* individuals are said to be related in two ways:

Moral units are groups of similar minds speaking the same language, having the same religion and arts, and stimulating by social sympathy and applause the genius native to their members. *Economic units,* on the contrary, are formed by the interdependence of dissimilar arts; they extend as far as do economic exchanges; they are unconscious systems of cooperation, like that which makes insects contribute to the reproduction of flowers.[52]

This distinction between moral and economic units is similar to that which Durkheim draws between mechanical and organic solidarity.[53] A moral unit, or moral society, is a community of persons united by custom and language, by mutual goals and consciousness of a common history and a common fate—factors which are, in *Reason in Society*, taken to be the prerequisites of free society. In saying that true society exists wherever there is analogous existence and community of ends, Santayana distinguishes what is later called a moral society, but it does not appear as a category in *Reason in Society*. In *Dominations and Powers* the language is characteristically unsystematic, but the categories are powerfully drawn, and moral societies are assigned a central role. They are included among the units represented by government and are the personification of moral freedom.[54]

Economic relations give rise to moral society but do not constitute it. A family, for example, is an economic unit, having a functional division of labor, and so on; Santayana says it becomes a moral entity by virtue of the ends and values its members come to share. In contrast, he does not consider the proletariat to be a moral society at all. Its members are distinguishable, Santayana says, not by any moral identity or mutuality, but by the absence of coherent ideals, by the rootlessness of a mass cut off from its history and its traditions. The only unity among proletarians, from a moral point of view, stems from their absolute equality: the equality of misery and what Santayana refers to as the "mystical" equality of naked spirits, characterized only by consciousness and "without attachments in any organic society, with no art, no religion, no friends, and no prospects."[55] Thus, we see the enormous moral importance he places on society, given his special definition of it. It should be noted that Santayana is distrustful of all new or transitory social movements; traditional society, traditional order are the only forms of society or order he accepts as legitimate. A people or race is defined by him as a community which is characterized by enduring and unanimous adherence to social norms and allegiance to the symbols of communal existence. While preserving the association of race with "blood," in *Dominations and Powers* Santayana refers to races as "moral societies." That is, whatever else a race may be, it is *at least* a moral society; and, for him, the *ultimate* ground of society is in physiology. But a moral society, for Santayana, involves more than just natural unanimity: even where custom and ritual are firmly established, individuals diverge spontaneously from accepted behavior patterns. In a moral society there is also a commitment to the unity of that society for its own sake and to a governing authority.[56]

The unity of a moral society is sharply contrasted by Santayana with the overwhelming but superficial unanimity that may be produced by propaganda or arise by contagion. It is the enduring unanimity and cooperativeness of "a family, or an army, or a philosophic sect, or religious community."[57] The dominant order in a moral society is provided by the channeling of motives which constitute major human concerns: generation and nutrition, love, protection, or the need for life to be meaningful—the interests governed by the system of social institutions. The *moral* essence of society, to which geography and politics (in the narrower sense) are irrelevant, is illustrated by Santayana with the case of the Jews, whom he cites as "a most wonderful instance of a people preserving its identity for two thousand years without any territorial possessions."[58] This identity is not that of an organism but takes the form of strong loyalty to a common cause, mutual understanding, voluntary cooperation, respect for a single authority, and consciousness of a common fate.

"The first principle of rationality in government" is "that it should protect and encourage vital liberty, in whatever quarter or form circumstances render its expression possible in action."[59] Vital liberty is the freedom of psyche, the integrity of vital energy in the individual. Metaphorically, Santayana extends it to moral societies as well, and his rational ideal, developed in terms of an individual society, is further extended to the government of an inclusive society: ". . . the very nature of rational economy could perfectly well extend its authority to other nations or even over the whole world."[60] Rational order at this level rests on the notion of the freedom of a society: since there is no liberty for Santayana in the absence of integrity, a society that is free could only be one in which there is firm discipline. Integrity in an individual is a function of constitution and habit; in a society it depends on tradition and is embodied in language and religion, custom and belief, and loyalty to the society itself. The vehicle of moral order, the locus of moral authority, is a moral society.

Government is called rational by Santayana when it is responsive to both psyche and circumstances: when it mediates between conflicting impulses, on the one hand, and between impulses and environmental forces, on the other. In other words, good government is government that is obedient to rational authority. To be rational, rulers would continually have to adjust the two effective, and hence authoritative, powers: the inertia of the generative order of society, as it is present in the body politic, and the impact of the natural (including the political) environment. No model of government is intrinsically rational, then; good government is an economic art, a perpetual effort to maintain equilibrium, not a specific constitution.[61]

It is the principle of rational authority which dictates that government shall promote the interest of the governed in the light of the best available knowledge since this is obedience to primal Will. The subjects of government, as Santayana sees it, are individual psyches and the moral societies which are at once their natural setting, their analogue, and the objects of their loyalty. The multiplicity and heterogeneity of moral agents (individuals or moral societies) in any society requires that government mediate among them, and between them and the world, to assure the greatest possible self-realization, the highest possible degree of self-determination or moral freedom, for each.

What is nominally called a country, as Santayana points out, is usually not a people, but a territory, inhabited by a number of tribes or ethnic and religious groups. The problem of freedom is, in part, that of fostering the development of culture, while maintaining the necessary political organization and preserving peace. To do this, Santayana holds, we must make historically evolved moral societies the units of political (economic, in its broad sense) order, maintaining a loose federation among them but never suppressing their cultural differences. He applies this model to both territorial and world government. The alternatives he sees are either to abandon the attempt to govern altogether and renounce freedom or to make moral societies such as those of Negroes, Catholics, or Jews secondary to the narrowly political order of society. In the latter case, he says, moral societies and civilization as we know it will wither and die.[62] This is the situation, he suggests, in the United States today, where it is just possible that a new moral society, although an impoverished one, is being created on the ashes of the multi-nation which was America.

NOTES

[1] *DP*, p. 297.

[2] *Ibid.*, p. 313.

[3] *Ibid.*, p. 316. ' We may note that it is impossible to specify antecedently whether an ideal is rational in this sense.

[4] *Ibid.*, p. 461.

[5] *RSoc*, p. 76.

[6] *DP*, p. 220.

[7] *RS*, p. 53; cf. also Santayana's "Introduction" to Spinoza's *Ethics* (New York: E.P. Dutton and Co., 1910), pp. xiv–xv.

[8] Cf. *DP*, p. 41, referred to in Chapter VII above.

[9] *DP*, pp. 421–22.

[10] *Ibid.*, p. 433.

[11] *RSoc*, pp. 75–76.

[12] *DP*, p. 315.

[13] *Ibid.*, p. 63.

[14] "Introduction" to Spinoza's *Ethics*, p. xiii.

[15] Benedict de Spinoza, *Political Treatise (op. posth.,* 1677), A. H. Gossett, trans., R. H. M. Elwes, ed., in *The Chief Works of Benedict de Spinoza,* I (New York: Dover Publications, Inc., 1955), p. 292.

[16] *DP*, p. 313.

[17] *Ibid.*

[18] *Ibid.*, p. 54.

[19] *Ibid.*, p. 60.

[20] Letter to John Hall Wheelock, August 30, 1950, *Letters*, p. 400.

[21] *DP*, p. 449.

[22] *Ibid.*, p. 25.

[23] Cf. *RA*, p. 32.

[24] *Ibid.*

[25] *Ibid.*, p. 17.

[26] *DP*, p. 91.

[27] *Ibid.*, p. 171.

[28] *PSL*, p. 286.

[29] *DP*, p. 149.

[30] *Ibid.*, p. 137.

[31] Cf. *Ibid.*, pp. 46–49.

[32] *Ibid.* p. 137.

[33] *Ibid.*, p. 151.

[34] *Ibid.*, p. 152.

[35] *Ibid.*, p. 10.

[36] *Ibid.*, p. 355.

[37] *Ibid.*, p. 51.

[38] Cf. *ibid.*, pp. 237, 242.

[39] *Ibid.*, p. 241.

[40] *Ibid.*, p. 60.

[41] *Ibid.*, pp. 187–88.

[42] *Ibid.*, p. 57.

[43] *Ibid.*, p. 240.

[44] *Ibid.*

[45] *Ibid.*, p. 450.

[46] *Ibid.*, p. 203.

[47] *Ibid.*, p. 14.

[48] *Ibid.*, p. 408. In the original the phrase refers to "a people," but the context and Santayana's general thesis concerning "moral units" justify its extension to any society.

[49] Eliseo Vivas, "From *The Life of Reason* to *The Last Puritan*," in *Philosophy*, pp. 313–50, cf. p. 339.

[50] Cf. *RSoc*, p. 133; *RSci*, pp. 258–59.

[51] Milton Karl Munitz, *The Moral Philosophy of Santayana* (1939), (reprint: New York: The Humanities Press, 1958), p. 51.

[52] *DP*, p. 443 (italics added).

[53] Emile Durkheim, *The Division of Labor in Society* (1893), George Simpson, trans. (New York: The Macmillan Company, 1933).

[54] In *Reason in Society* mention is made of "corporate individuals" (cf. p. 137); in *Dominations and Powers* Santayana speaks of "artificial organisms" (cf. p. 429), using the expression metaphorically to indicate the causal and dynamic nature of a moral society, while denying it, as a totality, any other organismic properties.

[55] *DP*, p. 368.

[56] Cf. *ibid.*, p. 429.

[57] *Ibid.*, p. 351.

[58] *Ibid.*, p. 452.

[59] *Ibid.*, p. 435.

[60] *Ibid.*

[61] Cf. *ibid.*, p. 382.

[62] Cf. *ibid.*, pp. 445–47.

CHAPTER 9

Santayana's Political Naturalism

SANTAYANA CONTRASTS his own ideal social order with those of Plato and Hegel, both of whom he thinks dictate the character moral society is to have, rather than merely specifying that those forms it assumes spontaneously are to be cultivated. In Hegel's State, psyches and moral societies are subordinated to the State itself. In Plato's Republic the forms of moral society are prescribed, and every facet of life from conception to contemplation is directed by fixed rules. Both are forms of autocracy which would stifle moral freedom. "The ideal to which they wished to sacrifice natural freedom was not the many-sided ideal radiation of spontaneous life, but a particular type of society or a particular method of change which they chose to impose on mankind or to attribute mythically to the universe."[1]

Like Plato's perfect society, however, and like Aristotle's and Hegel's ideals, Santayana's ideal commonwealth is defined by a moral purpose. Just as Plato's society is based on his definition of justice, Aristotle's on a conception of the good life, and Hegel's on the principle of Freedom, Santayana's ideal of a society governed according to the principle of rationality illustrates his own concept of moral freedom. A rational order of society would be "a liberal universal empire, under which every form of moral order might be developed by those communities to which it was native or congenial."[2]

Santayana's use of the term "liberal" here is deceptive, as I shall demonstrate. His idea of a rational social order is "liberal" only in one dimension. Such an order would be one in which moral societies flourish and are, instead of territorial divisions or the accidental arrangements stemming from military conquest, the accepted units of social organization. The Negroes, the Jews, and the Catholics (as well as the dominant white Protestants) in the United States, the Greeks and the Turks on the island of Cyprus, each of whom has what we might call ethnic identity, would, according to this plan, be encouraged to maintain their ethnicity. If they were permitted, Santayana believes, the members of these groups would draw closer together, perpetuate their special customs, and reinforce their private loyalties. They would preserve and continue to elaborate the symbols of their identity and their unique visions of the world. For Santayana, this would be a positive gain.

Adoption of the principle of moral freedom (the principle of spiritual wealth in spiritual liberty) is implicitly justified by Santayana on the basis of two considerations. First, in its purely ideal status as an essence, no type of organization may be said to be better or worse than any other. According to Santayana's version of naturalistic ethics, essences per se can only be evaluated in relation to an arbitrary standard. Secondly, piety to nature requires that effective powers be respected; they lend moral authority to their own ideal realizations. In the light of reason (mind) everything is what it is, and no private judgment is rationally justifiable. The source of all demands and all aspirations is equally natural, and the proper good of any form of life is the fulfillment of its own nature, regardless of any externally motivated judgment of that nature.

The principle of moral freedom is the principle that moral societies are to be kept "separate but equal." It would be easy to dismiss Santayana as a "racist," but the principle of moral freedom may be taken to do justice to actual conditions and to reflect a "moral truth." It is a sociological truism that, in a social group which has evolved its own norms, whose members are conscious of "belonging," the members identify their own destiny with that of the group and cling to their common identity. A class in power tends to assume that it is the ideal of every subordinate group to become as much like itself as possible; but this is not necessarily the case, as is eloquently demonstrated by the Black Power movement in the United States, by the struggle of French Canadians for recognition and power as a separate ethnic group, and by similar movements in other parts of the world. White Americans who reject Negro values and want Negroes to accept their own standards before granting them full equality are thereby, on Santayana's view, denying Negroes moral freedom. It is similarly the case that few workers wish to adopt the morality of the middle class, despite the assumptions of teachers and editorial writers. Santayana does not acknowledge the working class as a moral society because it has not developed what he considers to be a coherent moral tradition. On his own systematic grounds, I think he is wrong, although both the working class and other minorities in America may be in the process of altering their identity.

Despite the nominal equality he grants moral societies, Santayana would permit weaker societies to perish, for to protect one against another would be militant: the "wish to *reform* a decaying civilisation is itself singularly naive; it is fundamentally ignorant, under all the plumes and furbelows of a superficial omniscience."[3] Every civilization must, in its turn, be allowed to decay.

This doctrine implies that the generative order of nature, in supporting one policy or economy and defeating another, in effect establishes ethical and political criteria: strength = virtue, and power = right. Ultimately Santayana concludes that the only rational ideal can be to secure the fullest possible development of the actual forms of society that prevailing conditions allow. The function of government is to discover what this development would be and to act as a catalyst in its realization. Knowledge of the efficacious structures in society and nature is therefore requisite for rational government, which is consequently "scientific."[4]

Santayana recognizes that no man could possess the wide knowledge requisite for true rationality. The desire for rational government places us in the position of Socrates, perpetually reaching for more perfect self-knowledge and denying that good government is possible short of its attainment. The kernel of truth Santayana sees in the Socratic position is the principle that men should be governed in the light of the potentialities of their natures and their traditions and of the powers of nature at large to restrict or encourage them. Still, knowledge of what a rational order would be is no guarantee that the person possessing it will militantly prosecute the cause of that rational ideal—this requires moral involvement. And if such a person does commit himself to the attempt to institute even a rational ideal, he has not only ceased to be rational, in Santayana's terms: if there is a change in the society, that ideal of order may become a domination. Then, too, a rational order could not be sustained, even were an ideal philosopher to rule, for philosophers, like all other persons, are psyches, moral agents.[5] To rule the world a philosopher must live in it and must be animated by a vital concern. Once in the world he cannot help being caught up in the currents and controversies of real life. Thus, his outlook becomes parochial, moral, biased—and, ironically, wholesome. He is no longer governed by an impartial and scientific detachment but is committed and vitally interested. In short, in the attempt to introduce reason into politics, we must be content with limited aims and impermanent successes and resigned to a large measure of frustration. From this predicament the only real escape is through the imagination, in the contemplation of ideals which, though they may be unrealizable, mitigate the cruelty of existence.

Sabine criticizes Santayana for failing to make a place in the conceptual framework of *Dominations and Powers* for what the anthropologists call culture.[6] Santayana does not employ the term in its current technical sense but typically uses it honorifically to refer to the products of liberal art and their appreciation by privileged individuals. But if by "culture" we mean the "historically created designs for living, explicit and implicit, rational, irrational, and non-rational, which exist at any given time as potential guides for the behavior of men,"[7] it is precisely to culture that Santayana looks for the necessary conditions of human freedom. The essence of the notion of many nations in one empire is that every people is to retain its own culture, its historically developed identity, and imperial force is only to be employed to maintain peace among them when this is judged to be necessary. It may be repeated that this is not meant to express a militant ideal; peace is not to be maintained at any price, and the objective is not peace itself, but the preservation and development of naturally evolved races or nations. Neither the government in power nor the critical philosopher is permitted to dictate to anyone concerning the value of any tradition or belief.

From the point of view of their existence and their special character or culture, the moral societies which are the building blocks of the rational order are not themselves rational, for in Santayana's view, the generative order of nature, to which both psyche and society belong, is "irrational." That is, from the point of view of human needs and human reason it is chaotic and purposeless; there is no reason that we can discover in nature itself for it to have the particular character that it does. We could distinguish this as *ontological* irrationality. In this sense, rational authority is, paradoxically, the authority of the irrational or, more properly, of the non-rational. To the extent that they are well organized, however, and well adjusted to circumstances, moral societies may be said to be *morally* rational and to have what Santayana calls a rational economy. Societies which are rational in this way are the members of the ideal empire.

Santayana envisages a situation in which self-determination is made possible for a multitude of moral societies by the existence of traditional (i.e., "natural") order in each and scientific supervision of their economies and their mutual relations. A rational, supra-national government would be concerned with the natural, not the moral, economy of each nation—that is, it would govern its relations to the physical world and to other nations, leaving the direction of its cultural and political development "to the special genius of each free society and each free individual."[8] It must be remembered that, according to Santayana, each free individual and society is free only by virtue of the way its energies are channelled and adjusted. Vital liberty is a harmony of forces, not an antecedent condition—it is an achievement, not a gift or a right. Freedom is consequent upon discipline; it follows for Santayana that "a state of society and a discipline of the will inspired by pure reason would be neither romantic nor liberal. It would be sternly organic, strictly and traditionally moral, military, and scientific."[9] In the absence of strict discipline, as he sees it, social relations are confused and inconsistent, and psyche is distracted. A rational government, therefore, would not leave the moral order to chance. It would deliberately cultivate existing societies and their institutions, helping them adjust to their physical and political environment. In this way it "would speak for the material conditions imposed by nature on the realisation of any ideal without dictating to any person or society what its ideal should be."[10] Thus, it would be obedient to the authority of both psyche and circumstances. But each psyche and moral society must be strictly governed, and a rational government of a compound society would be "liberal" only in that it would be charitable toward the different types of thoroughgoing order it encompassed.

It would seem that if the spontaneous and overwhelming movement of a people is in the direction of change, a government which serves tradition would be militant and autocratic. Santayana himself states that while rational government "should be steady and traditional," it should also be "open to continual readjustments with the natural shift of customs, passions, and aspirations in the world."[11] One senses that Santayana identifies order primarily with tradition because he associates change with chaos. On Santayana's grounds, a chaotic society could not be free, for it would lack integrity. A society in revolution has destroyed the order which characterized it, has overthrown the norms which unified it, and can no longer be a moral society. Nothing without "form" can be said to be. This is the basis of the importance Santayana attributes to the realm of essence. As it is for Plato, for Santayana a thing's form or nature is its proper good. Civilization and tradition are the form, the *arête* of society. They make for definiteness of perspective and distinction in ideals and are requisite for the rise of leadership, as well as for art, religion, and morality. Civilization is, like psyche, a kind of "entelechy," a form which life strives to maintain and which therefore constitutes the standard according to which Santayana would evaluate every polity.

The rational order of society is defined by the concept of rational government, not by the design of its economy, thus precluding a fixed system such as that advocated by socialists or communists. Santayana also prohibits the imposition of the liberal formula for the realization of freedom. Liberals believe, with him, that government should not impose political, moral, or intellectual ideologies on any one. The liberal doctrine states that only the safety of person and property is to be regulated, "while in everything intellectual or ideal each man should bravely paddle his own canoe."[12] Liberals hold, in addition, that beliefs and obligations, values and preferences are individual concerns and ought not be subject to societal control. But Santayana contends that beliefs, tastes, and norms are social, not purely individual products, and that the very freedoms which liberals hold dear are coercions and determine the values that will prevail in society. Free trade, private property, universal education, the separation of church and state, all of which they would institute in the name of liberty, are determinate forms of social organization and generate their own norms, values, and ideals. The moral economy which liberals propose is, therefore, as much a "material social bondage" as any other and enslaves the mind in the same way. Nature does not allow the sort of "division of labor" the liberals would establish in the moral economy, because the ideas and ideals men generate do not have a life of their own but reflect the motives, the lives, and the circumstances of those who conceive them. It is the "material" organization of psyches and social institutions, rather than the laws which supposedly govern them, which, according to Santayana, determine the moral and intellectual life of men and the character and quality of their civilizations.

Spirit has and can have no other constancy than that of its organ: if the organ is fluid or ephemeral, the thought and feeling that belong to it will drift like a cloud. When, on the contrary, the organ finds a firm lodgment in the body politic, when the free association takes root in society, the government may disregard the thing officially, but the private body will become in fact a second government, a part of that officious social order which really dominates mankind.[13]

The more elaborate and definite the social order is, the more varied and clearly articulated will be the landscape discernible by spirit, and the more firmly attached psyche will be to those ideals which represent its true good; i.e., the more rigorous the discipline it imposes, the greater the spiritual freedom society creates and, at the same time, the firmer the foundation for vital liberty. The price of liberty is constraint.

Santayana had adopted this view quite early, pointing out in an essay "Liberalism and Culture," written in 1915, that government according to the *professed* principles of liberalism, were it possible, would have precluded the development of those institutions which establish moral order and provide the substance of imaginative life.[14] It is only because liberalism arose after the fixation of traditions that it could occasionally be viable and beneficial by loosening the constraints of dead conventions. But in so far as it pretends to be grounded in "truths" about human nature and society, Santayana holds the liberal doctrine to be false. A rational moral economy, in contrast to one that is "liberal" in this sense, would have to be a conservative one in which government preserves and protects the factors making for social order and coherence, the traditions which comprise the distinctive identity of each society. The government which controls the destiny of a society must cultivate the patterns of behavior which are customary in that society in order to maintain the foundations of those beliefs and allegiances which lend meaning to its life.

It will be recalled that the rational order of society has two distinguishable, but inseparable, dimensions.[15] The first is the establishment of an optimal relation of necessary and liberal arts, providing the greatest possible freedom in the spiritual economy, the widest scope for intrinsically rewarding activity and for the creation and appreciation of symbols of the ideal. The second factor in the rational order is the balanced relation between government and moral societies. The possibility of a liberal employment of energy is contingent upon the success of the economic arts; the more efficient an economy becomes, the more rational it will be. "The moral function of economic art," Santayana says, "is to enlarge vital liberty."[16] In a rational society men will spontaneously adhere to, and freely articulate, the symbols, values, and ideals of that society. But liberal art cannot be produced by one man at the command of another; nor will great art, on Santayana's view, be produced if the artist tries to portray an ideal which he does not truly understand, which does not express his own vital impulses. Spiritual freedom and liberal art presuppose both moral or political freedom and economic order.

This does not mean that only the economy, in the narrow sense of this term, is to be regulated, and the rest of social life is to be ungoverned. A rational *moral* economy (a rational "division of moral labor") is said to be one in which government maintains "order where the conditions are known" but permits "liberty where imagination makes its own laws."[17] On the epiphenomenalist hypothesis, imagination makes no laws but is dependent upon bodily life. Santayana seems to mean that existing social order is to be strengthened and assisted and that the role of government is not to impose new ends or even new means, but to cope with those environmental factors which affect the continuing operation of the social system. Government should, in the light of knowledge of nature and society, control the factors which could frustrate the satisfaction of the real needs of those under its jurisdiction—this would be government "for the people." But to the degree consistent with this policy, government should refrain from interfering with the moral choices or the customary practices and beliefs of tightly organized psyches and societies. Government's task is therefore primarily economic. "Economic arts" are those activities which consist in turning nature—whether this be physical or social nature—to human ends. Where nature is not amenable to change, it is rational to modify one's goals. To some extent, then, it would seem impossible to avoid interference with moral freedom.

Sabine finds Santayana's dislike of liberalism unintelligible in view of his belief that Santayana's ideal of freedom is similar to the liberal ideal:

What he desires that rational authority should bring about is really very little different from what liberal democracy hoped for: a government fully informed, sympathetic and understanding toward all valid claims of social and private interest, and tolerant of wide variations in the tastes and aspirations of individuals and social groups, or in the words of John Stuart Mill, a society which sincerely believes "that the free de- velopment of individuality is one of the leading essentials of well-being."[18]

But as Santayana believes that the essence of individuality is limitation and the existence of a moral society is determined by the development of institu- tions, their free development, for him, can only be consequent upon the per- sistence of the social order. The stricter that order and the more closely it is integrated into the wider natural order in which it has its life, the more free- dom has been achieved. The function of government is both to serve and to keep order. Hence the establishment of a rational economy presupposes a "strict and 'totalitarian' discipline within the rational circle."[19] This is the perspective in which Santayana's critique of liberalism is understandable. The nations of Santayana's empire are rigorously governed moral societies. As he sees it, if the liberal prescription were really followed by any people, even at this stage in history, discipline would lapse and, with it, commitment to firmly established values and ends; militant leaders would then become nuclei of faction, and moral order be destroyed by sectarian conflict.

"Moral realities must have a physical basis; and, through their physical basis, they may become competitive."[20] In the light of reason, all ideals are equally valid, and, as possibilities, all ideals may coexist without conflict. But the organisms or societies which embody different forms and strive for different goals (and compete, in some cases, for the same living space), may conflict in the crush of physical life. Moral society can never be universal; individual motivation itself is complex, and the demands of innumerable individuals, added to the diversity of moral societies, make it impossible to allow any one "vacant freedom." The problem of rational politics is to dis- cover just that kind and degree of order in the moral economy which will provide maximum freedom, to establish as far as possible a "peace between order and liberty."[21] *Ideally* (as we have seen, this is an impossible goal), the domains of order and liberty should be distinct: government should control the external circumstances and the instrumental pursuits which condition liberal activity and make it possible or, when government fails, frustrate and inhibit it. Government should regulate the relations of individuals and soci- eties to one another and to nature at large, but it should allow individuals and moral societies freedom in the choice of ends, which is moral freedom. A federal or an international government must remain impartial. Otherwise, in committing itself to one or another people, it becomes irrational and is no longer the moral representative of all nations of the empire. If it is to intro- duce rational order and to insure the existence of conditions under which

freedom may be realized, government must harmonize the diversity of existing interests, as well as reconcile them with surrounding forces. Thus, the
rational interest in harmony reappears in *Dominations and Powers,* not as
an expression of moral idealism or of a commitment to harmony as a good in
itself, but as a means of adjustment to authoritative circumstances on the part
of existing societies.

In imposing any conditions upon the governed, even in the name of circumstances, Santayana says, a ruler is autocratic, i.e., militant and dicta-
torial. But government that was not in some degree militant would not be
government at all. A part of the irony of government is that while its purpose
is to maintain peace, it is necessarily in itself a species of war since there can
be no government without enforcement of the ruler's policies.[22] The government of an empire, in contrast to that of a moral society, ought not be "totalitarian"; that is, it ought not to impose a uniform moral order on the diverse
societies under its rule.[23] Santayana's desire to safeguard moral diversity is
the ground of his condemnation of the egalitarian ideal of perfect democracy.
He applies the name "spontaneous democracy" to a moral society of a special sort, where a natural unanimity and sense of unity have come to exist
"unintended and unopposed, in the generative order of society, by a broth-
erly identity of impulse and interest, like that of crawling cubs in a litter, a
concord which rivalry has not yet disturbed."[24] But because this unity arises
in a universe in which spontaneous impulses clash and numberless powers
contend, faction is bound to disturb it sooner or later, and natural democracies are short-lived. It is possible to retain the machinery of democracy in a
society thus become political, but unanimity in policy and in action can only
be sustained, under these conditions, by the elimination or suppression of
individuals who no longer share the sense of participation in a common
enterprise and a common destiny. The ideal of a perfect ultimate democracy
is consequently, for Santayana, as absolutist as any other sectarian ideal.
The ideological democrat assumes that a natural unanimity exists, and
believes that men should become one in their ideal commitments and thereby
wholly cooperative and sympathetic. Santayana denies this on the ground
that actual tendencies in the generative order of society render the ideal of
unanimity tyrannical. The democratic ideal is not an ideal of freedom.

"Vital liberty differentiates. Only vacant freedom leaves all in the same
anonymous crowd."[25] Instead of liberty, democratic doctrinaires would
impose "an always contemporary absolute in an always different unanimity
of mankind, to be secured by the continual suppression of minorities."[26] The
most extreme example of an attempt to impose a utopian democracy is,
according to Santayana, communism. But he sees in the history of the United

States the same imposition of uniformity being accomplished by different means. Whereas the Soviets employ coercion, the Americans use education and the promise of material comfort in order to suppress racial and class differences. Both regimes may succeed, and in both countries, says Santayana, citizens may become convinced that the "all-pervasive authority" under which they live is perfect freedom since they can no longer conceive or desire a different way of life.[27] Santayana's own ideal differs from this in that the all-pervasive authority is traditional and not political (in either the wider or the narrower sense); and a multiplicity of rigidly disciplined moral orders, rather than a single order, would prevail within a political unit. He would not deny that this is a kind of servitude but would take it to be necessary, or at least unavoidable.

In the meantime in America, according to Santayana, unanimity remains to be won; yet should it ever be established, despite the sacrifice of moral diversity, he feels America might develop into a great nation. A truly potent society would be one with a firm and elaborate tradition and strong and consistent leadership. Its promise was not fulfilled, but before the end of World War II, when its president had been kept in office for a fourth term, the scope of governmental control had been vastly extended, and its political direction seemed stable and coherent, Santayana says he believed the government of the United States had become an "intelligent" and "automatic power." He thought it was on the way to becoming a great and "traditional" government like that of ancient Rome.[28] By virtue of its strength, he suggests, such a government could have ruled the United Nations and the world, now without effective government, the U.N. being, in his eyes, only the battleground of sovereign interests, without integrity or power in its own right. "A universal government would have to be a particular government, rooted in the generative order of history, and not an alliance of sovereign states or a universal parliament."[29] The universality of that government, if it were to be rational, could not be that of a monolithic state; a rational government would not turn the world into a single moral society. But if it retained its own integrity, Santayana hopes, a powerful, stable, and intelligent government might rule an empire like that of the Romans without depriving its tributary societies of their moral freedom.

It seems clear that Santayana personally despises both proletarian equality and the American ideal of a "competitive society of perfectly educated and legally disciplined equals."[30] It is also apparent that, in the perspective of moral relativism, a democracy of either sort, if imposed from above, represents as foreign and tyrannical an ideal as a dictatorship similarly enforced. But the essence of political democracy is self-government, which would, on the face of it, seem to be the best way to insure moral freedom (self-determination). Santayana does accept the rationality of self-government for those natural democracies which flower occasionally. But they are rare and temporary. In a heterogeneous political unit many people would find it reasonable to think that if every moral society could have a spokesman in government, the interests of all would be represented. But, Santayana asserts, such a government would be haphazard, its decisions determined by the pressure of competing powers, not by reason. Parliamentary government deteriorates into government by politics and comes to represent, not the interests of the governed, but their clashing opinions.[31] Government by politics betrays the public interest by pandering to the directive imagination of both the public and its representatives, allowing the question of the interest of the governed to be decided by oratory and political pressure, not by science. Rational government, in contrast, is government by a ruler who is interested in the welfare of the governed and is wise enough to discern what this interest is and how it can be promoted.

Although a country comprising several moral societies may not be unanimous in its loyalties or its needs, in so far as it *is* a community, Santayana holds it to have a single interest. Class conflict, if it stems from real diversity of interests, would mean to him that there is no true society. And if supposed class or party differences are not genuine, then party politics is a sham battle, and party platforms are mere sophistry. If the interest of a society is in some sense unitary for Santayana, it is also "ideal" in a special sense, for it is only in a mind that he thinks the required synthesis of competing interests and forces allegedly representing the good of all can occur. "The common good" is considered by Santayana to be a fiction. Rational government is, from this point of view, a method of imaginative synthesis. He concludes that government is properly to be directed by a single individual: "Occasional aggregates like governments and societies cannot be rationally guided except by the mind of a single individual."[32] The model of rational government, therefore, is "monarchy," by which Santayana seems to mean something like "benevolent despotism," autocratic control which, by organizing cooperation, assists a varied multiplicity of moral beings in the effort to coexist and still flourish as individuals.

Rational government cannot be established once for all by the adoption of a constitution, for moral societies change and so does the world. Even where law expresses tradition and is therefore authoritative, it cannot be permanently rational because it is static and inherently partial. The interest of a people, or, in the case of world government, of all peoples, must constantly be reappraised.

Santayana is aware that the sort of moral representation which an ideal monarchy would exemplify is unrealizable. But strangely, he fails to see the

defects of individual rule even considered purely as an ideal. On his epiphenomenalist theory, it is hard to see how a mental synthesis could be trans-
lated into action or even be purposively effected.[33] Even if it could, he
provides insufficient grounds for the judgment that a synthesis formulated by
a single thinker is more adequate to the needs of the governed, or more
expressive of their Will, than a synthesis hammered out in the courts or in
the legislature. For even if a monarch were not self-seeking, he would necessarily, by virtue of his individuality, be biased. Neither does Santayana
demonstrate that the Will of the people, their "true" interest, is, in fact, *one*
in any but a purely verbal sense. Even if the interest in self-realization is
universal, the means for its attainment are many. Especially in view of the
inevitable limitation of human knowledge, there seems to be no justification
for the claim that harmony after the pattern conceived by one man is to be
preferred to harmony reached by another road.

But the more important—and more substantial—part of Santayana's
treatment of the problem of a rational social order is his prescription of a
pluralistic system under an "imperial" authority. In this connection, he
seems not to have considered that, if it were to inspire loyalty, any social
order would have to be a moral society, even if, as in this case, it would be a
moral society of a special sort. In a pluralistic society, many attachments and
many loyalties command allegiance, and if there is no inclusive community,
there is no shared ideal in terms of which conflict can be resolved—there is
no motive for its resolution. The mere desire for peace, on Santayana's
assumptions, is impotent to bring about a rapprochement between conflicting powers. And it often happens that existing motives making for conflict
are stronger than those making for agreement. As Santayana sees it, the task
of government in such a case is to bring about the kind of peace that will in-
fringe as little as possible upon the private loyalties of the contending
parties. But we can see that if there is no commitment to that government
itself or to the order it stands for, the powers in question will be unwilling
to sacrifice their autonomy.

Moral society is characterized by the tendency to cling to traditional
beliefs, standards, and ideals. In itself this would be an obstacle to the institution of a new, inclusive community, however minimal its requirements. But
the major obstacle to the kind of order Santayana envisions is the tendency on
the part of certain groups to try to dominate or convert others. Santayana
himself takes aggressiveness, or primal Will, to be the definitive characteristic of animal life and sees the inevitable bias of Will turning primal spontaneity into militancy. Thus, individuals or societies may persist in mutually frus-
trating activities and, as a result of conflict, may become intolerant of one
another. Beyond this, they may be so intent on realizing their own purposes

that they try to turn everything they encounter to their own ends. A militant Will would be strongly motivated and difficult to divert. If, as Santayana holds, we cannot employ reason to introduce new motives, the only way to redirect a militant Will would be to use force. He grants that whole societies can be moved to action by "contagion" but denies that such influence can be either long-lasting or controlled. But when government imposes unity by force, it alienates those whom it is trying to bind together in a common enterprise.

Given a multiplicity of moral societies whose members have no society in common, the problem is to produce solidarity among them. Moral society, for Santayana, is the product of a common history. The nations of the world may be said to have a common past, but they have no common history or tradition and no common body of beliefs and practices. Santayana does not solve the problem of providing them with a common goal.

Santayana calls attention to the importance of ideals in human life, but his epiphenomenalism makes it difficult to account for this importance. The very "ideality" of the symbols of religion, art, politics, and inquiry deprives them of efficacy. They are portrayed as expressions and foci of aspiration and loyalty, but Santayana cannot explain how they *inspire* affective response. And if ideals as such cannot inspire loyalty, it is hard to see how moral society could be deliberately instituted. Santayana attributes the apparent influence of rhetoric to physical "contagion" and association but, in so doing, only postpones answering the central question: how are symbols meaningful? If ideas cannot move men, not only are we hampered in the effort to govern but ideas themselves have been stripped of significance.

Santayana's ideal commonwealth is conceived as a way of comprehending numerous existing moral societies in a unity, having as its primary aim the maintenance of the diversity and distinctiveness of its components. The government of such an empire must maintain peace among its members. But primal Will in each individual (and, analogously, in each society) inevitably comes into conflict with Will in some other embodiment. A necessary condition of Santayana's ideal would be that conflicting Wills be ready to compromise their differences. The alternative would be for one to conquer the other. The consequence of either course would seem to be a net loss of individuality. By temperament, Santayana appears to prefer the second; but to do so is to abandon the pluralistic ideal. However, he suggests, before any society could swallow up the whole world, other societies would arise and enrich the world by the addition of new cultures. To a detached spirit, a succession of different forms of life is as satisfying as their coexistence; the only standard Santayana refuses to abandon is the standard of diversity per se. The justification he offers for his adoption of this standard is that diversity actually occurs in the natural world. But if a single power did succeed in dominating all others, Santayana would be able to provide no rational basis for opposing it.

Santayana considers existence in itself to be meaningless and sees no purpose or general progress in history. In *Reason in Science* he describes one way of adjusting to this concept of existence. Christianity and other disillusioned and post-rational religions posit a transcendent meaning, developing elaborate and beautiful visions in terms of which life can be seen to be purposive and ethical systems justified. Santayana takes any such view of existence to reflect the needs of its originator: it has its roots in the generative order of nature. But, in placing the good outside the realm of natural existence, religion is not rational. Santayana's interpretation of history and society in *Dominations and Powers* is disillusioned but not "post-rational." It represents his lifelong attempt to explain the meaning and the justification of moral and political ideals in relation to their source, and introduces a political ideal which is "rational" in a new sense: granted that there is no reason in existence per se, Santayana seeks to base his ideal on the meanings and values that arise *within* the context of social life. Such an ideal is rational in the sense of being obedient to rational authority: relevant to existing cultures and to compelling circumstances and approachable, if not fully realizable. It is justified by the conditions of the actual world, not by an arbitrary standard.

Dominations and Powers, even more than *The Life of Reason,* reflects the irony in Santayana's perception of the human condition, the tension he sees between liberty and order, between vitality and the need for government, and between reason and tradition. Men create ideals out of profound need and then act as if their ideal creations, the imagined fulfillment of their deepest desires, were actual and causal. That is, they become idolators. For, on Santayana's "materialist" assumptions, ideals are inefficacious, and religion and philosophy are helpless to influence the course of events.

Political ideologies are similarly impotent for Santayana and suffer the additional defect of reflecting transitory and merely situational conditions. Unlike politics, science has been able to transform the surface of the earth, but only to the extent that scientists have been able to discover and conform to the underlying order of nature.[34] To be effective, government must be "scientific," not "ideological"; but it must be an economic, not in any sense a liberal, art. Science itself, according to Santayana, is a liberal art; its applications are economic. Government ought to be an applied science: it should be based on the facts of social life and should respect established institutions, not introduce a social order based on abstract preference. Rulers may not promulgate ideals but must pay homage to the traditional order of society. This is the role of reason in government.

Santayana sees the whole meaning of human life in its ideals and the entire purpose of government in the protection of cultural distinction. The most profound irony in his picture of human life is this paradox in the function of ideals: they express the powers that motivate man, and, in so doing, they reveal him to himself; in this expressive role and in their sheer aesthetic quality they make life worthwhile. But they are without practical value since they are neither powers nor instrumentalities whereby man can control either his conduct or his circumstances. Santayana explains the fact that people with different beliefs conduct themselves differently by saying that the conduct determines the beliefs, not the beliefs the conduct. As a result, he is not simply pessimistic about the possibility of controlling human conduct by suggesting new aims: he emphatically repudiates such an enterprise as a case of egotism.

In proposing his own societal ideal, Santayana asserts that he would not institute a transformation of society. In this sense, he does not prescribe a new ideal or present a design for a perfect society. Instead, he would foster the well-being of existing societies, preserving their native character. Even a government with such a limited purpose would, to the extent that its goal was fixed, be militant and egotistical. But without government we would regress to "life in the jungle," and in the absence of militancy, life would reduce to blind and purposeless drift.

NOTES

[1] *DP*, p. 392.

[2] *Ibid.*, p. 453.

[3] *Ibid.*, p. 438.

[4] *Ibid.*, p. 434.

[5] *Ibid.*, p. 428.

[6] George H. Sabine, *op. cit.*, p. 402.

[7] Clyde Kluckhohn and William Kelly, "The Concept of Culture," in Ralph Linton, ed., *The Science of Man in the World Crisis* (New York: Columbia University Press, 1945), p. 97.

[8] *DP*, p. 463.

[9] *Ibid.*, p. 158.

[10] *Ibid.*, p. 435.

[11] *Ibid.*, p. 382.

[12] *Ibid.*, p. 352.

[13] *Ibid.*, p. 451. The word "material" has the same connotation in the following: "As a form of life and action the practice of any art enters into the

vortex of material social currents that aid or impede one another in the world." *Ibid.*, p. 433.

[14] *SE*, pp. 173–78.

[15] Cf. Chapter VIII above.

[16] *DP*, p. 91.

[17] *Ibid.*, p. 463.

[18] George H. Sabine, *op. cit.*, pp. 406–7.

[19] *DP*, p. 296. Santayana's use of the word "totalitarian" is inconsistent. It does not seem to be, for him, a technical term.

[20] *Ibid.*, p. 443.

[21] *Ibid.*, p. 463.

[22] *Ibid.*, p. 79.

[23] *Ibid.*, p. 435.

[24] *Ibid.*, p. 344.

[25] *Ibid.*, p. 358.

[26] *Ibid.*, p. 351.

[27] *Ibid.*, pp. 347–48.

[28] *Ibid.*, p. 458.

[29] *Ibid.*, p. 456.

[30] *Ibid.*, p. 348.

[31] Cf. *ibid.*, p. 309.

[32] *Ibid.*, p. 372.

[33] Cf. *RCS*, p. 215: " . . . the world is an unaccountable datum, in its existence, in its laws, and in its incidents. The highest hopes of science and morality look only to discovering those laws and bringing one set of incidents—facts of perception—into harmony with another set—facts of preference. This hoped-for issue, if it comes, must come about in the mind; but the mind cannot be its cause since, by hypothesis, it does not possess the ideas it seeks nor has the power to realise the harmonies it desiderates. These have to be waited for and begged of destiny. . . ."

[34] It should be recalled that Santayana does not consider nature intrinsically intelligible, but holds that the regularities we experience must be taken to indicate an order beneath—a cosmos which accounts for this experience.

Index

Action, 13–15, 54, 108
Actuality, 65, 68
Adjustment, 48, 61, 64, 101, 103, 108, 113
Animal faith, 17, 23
Appearance, 22–23
Aristocracy, 13, 64
Aristotle, 1, 2, 5, 21, 33, 39, 62, 63
Art, 2, 14, 36, 38, 65–66, 84, 95, 111, 112, 125, 133. *See also* Economic art; Liberal art
Atomism, 54, 55, 115
Authority, 90–91, 99n, 115, 118, 130. *See also* Rational authority
Autocracy, 97–98, 121, 125, 129
Automatism, 13, 28–29, 33, 79, 83

Bacon, F., 92
Benedict, R., 51
"Blood," 47, 48, 50, 55, 117
Body, 20–21
Buchler, J., 45, 61
Burke, E., 3

Carthage, 92
Catholicism, 82, 118, 121
Causation, 11, 12, 18–19, 27, 28
Chance, 12
Chaos, 12–13, 125
Character, 41, 46, 49
Charity, 60, 70–71, 114, 124
China, 106
Chivalry, 72
Christianity, 6, 95, 97–98, 134
Church, the, 92
Circumstances, 63, 64, 90, 102. *See also* Rational authority
Civilization, 32, 35, 36, 46, 48, 61, 72, 80, 115, 125
Commitment, 75, 91, 105, 117, 123, 132
Common good, 131
Common sense, 3, 19, 21, 23–24, 66, 90
Communication, 53–55 *passim*

Communism, 92, 125
Community, 46, 72, 131, 132
Competition, 80, 81
Conflict, 68, 71, 80, 81, 105, 131–33 *passim*
Conquest, 34, 105–6, 121, 133
Consciousness, 2, 20–23 *passim*, 65, 68, 83, 86, 108. *See also* Epiphenomenalism; Mind; Spirit; Thought
Conservatism, 3, 64, 85, 90, 126
Constitutional government, 131
Corporate individuals, 37, 54, 120n
Cosmos, 27, 30–33
Criticism, 66
Culture, 46, 48, 49, 51, 59, 80, 118, 123–24, 135
Custom, 33, 34, 64, 80, 90, 117

Democracy, 35, 73, 86, 95, 129–31
Democritus, 28, 100n
Dennes, W. R., 24–25
Detachment, 7, 114, 123
Determinism, 13
Dewey, J., 17, 27, 39
Dialectical science, 4, 5, 27
Directive imagination, 94, 131
Discipline, 64, 75, 113, 117, 124–28 *passim*
Discourse, 26
Disillusion, 6, 60, 73–74, 95, 101, 134
Diversity, 64, 68–70 *passim*, 76n, 113, 118, 129, 133–34
Dogmatism, 66
Domination(s), 4, 70, 84, 85, 88, 96, 97, 104–6 *passim*, 113
Durkheim, E., 116

Earlier and later views, Chapter 3 *passim*, Chapter 6 *passim*, 78, 92
Economic art, 96, 109, 111, 127, 134
Economic determinism, 32
Efficacy, 26, 27, 29, 35, 83, 84

Egotism, 63, 93–95, 135
Egypt, 51
Empiricism, 24, 29, 94
Ends, 2, 6, 37–38, 42, 68
English, the, 49
Enterprise, 81, 82
Epiphenomenalism, 14–15, Chapter 3 *passim*, 47–48, 55, 59, 65, 83, 113–14, 127, 132, 133, 136*n*
Equality, 130
Essences, 2, 3, 22, 26, 37–39 *passim*, 122
Ethical naturalism, 89, 122. *See also* Moral naturalism
Ethics, 5–6, 60, 63–64, 66–67, 86, 106. *See also* Ethical naturalism; Morality; Moral naturalism
Evolution, 33, 51, 55, 72
Existence, 10–11, 18, 21, 25, 29, 33, 89, 101, 113, 134
Experience, 10, 15, 18, 20–22 *passim*, 28–29, 41, 57
Explanation, 28
External objects, 22–23, 28

Fact, 10–11, 27
Faction, 128, 129
Family, 32–35 *passim*, 37, 40, 43, 56, 64, 116
Fanaticism, 43, 81, 85
Fascism, 51, 92
Fatalism, 14
Faurot, J. J., 1
Federal government, 118, 128–29
Feudal society, 35
Flux, 33, 38, 39, 42, 65
Form, 13, 25–26, 29, 33, 44*n*, 125
Free society, 32, 36, 37, 40, 42, 47, 82, 117, 124
Freedom, 14, 43–44, 46, 63, 74, 75, 79, 80, 86, 107–18 *passim*, Chapter 9 *passim*. *See also* Liberty; Moral freedom; Spiritual freedom; Vacant freedom; Vital liberty
Free will, 108
Fromm, E., 50

Generative order of society, 78–80, 84, 111
Germans, the, 95
German philosophy, 94

Given, the, 65
God, 26, 39, 114
Good, 4, 5, 36, 70, 71, 86–87, 88–89, 104, 134. *See also* Value
Good government, 69, 85, 86, 118. *See also* Moral representation; Rational authority; Rational government
Gospels, the, 111
Government, 32–35 *passim*, 37, 38, 41, 69, 70, 79, 82, 87, 92, 97–98, 105, 111, 113, 127–35 *passim*. *See also* Constitutional government; Good government; Parliamentary government; Rational government; Representative government; World government
Greeks, the, 48, 49, 62–63, 68, 97, 103

Habit, 33, 64
Harmony, 61, 64, 65, 68, 74, 101, 102, 128–29
Hegel, G. W. F., 97, 121
Heresy, 95
Hinduism, 82
History, 10, 13, 33, 95, 96, 101, 134
Hume, D., 5
Human condition, 108, 134
Humanity, 40
Human nature, 38, 51, 55, 64, 68, 69, 76*n*, 85, 126

Idealism, 25
Ideality, 4, 37, 109–10, 133
Ideal realization, 3, 38, 96
Ideal ruler, 87. *See also* Moral representation
Ideals, 2, 4–5, 13, 26, 37, 38, 41, 60–62, 65, 68, 71, 81, 89, 91, 103, 106–7, 110, 115, 123, 126, 128, 133–35 *passim*. *See also* Ideality; Ideal realization; Moral idealism; Moral ideals; Political ideals; Utopian ideals
Ideal society, 22, 32, 38–40, 65–66
Ideas, 13, 26, 38–40, 65, 85, 126. *See also* Actuality; Appearance; External objects; Ideal society; Objects; Reality
Ideology, 12, 85, 87, 134
Idolatry, 47, 134
Impartiality, 89, 114, 123
Impulse, 70, 102
Individualism, 52–55 *passim*, 68, 90

Individuality, 34, 46, 55, 71, 73, 128
Industrial revolution, 83
Industrial societies, 112
Industry, 32, 37, 41, 82, 84, 111
Inertia, 88, 104
Innovation, 81, 84
Inquiry, 82, 133
Instinct, 34, 48, 56, 79
Instinctive society, 34, 41
Instrumentalism, 27
Integrity, 51, 63, 72, 115, 117-18
Intellect, 30n, 36, 67, 79
Intelligence, 15, 54, 61, 102, 113
Intelligibility, 26-28 passim, 101, 136n 33, 136n 34
Intent, 82, 83
Interest, 3, 43, 64, 69, 71, 73, 104, 106, 131
Irrationality, 27, 28, 64, 74, 75, 124

Jews, the, 49, 82, 95, 117, 118, 121
Justice, 72

Kant, I., 2, 18-19, 21, 76n, 77n, 94
Kluckhohn, C., 50
Knowledge, 1, 15, Chapter 3 passim, 30n, See also Thought

Language, 47, 53-55, 101, 111
Laski, H., 73
Law, 90
Laws of nature, 13, 33
Legitimacy, 91-92, 106
Lenin, V. I., 88
Liberal art, 109-12, 127, 134
Liberalism, 3, 73, 80, 86, 121, 125-28
Liberty, 71, 107-18 passim. See also Freedom; Moral freedom; Vital liberty
Life of Reason, 32, 36, 60-62, 101-2, 110
Love, 32, 41
Loyalty, 132

Machiavelli, N., 92, 93, 96
Man, 2
Mankind, 39
Many Nations in One Empire, 109, 124
Materialism, 3, Chapter 2 passim, Chapter 3, 42, 49-50, 60, 61, 66-67, 70, 79, 83, 107, 126, 134

Mathematics, 101
Matter, Chapter 3 passim, 44n, 65, 79
Mead, G. H., 52-55
Mechanism, 13, 25, 27-28, 33, 42, 64, 83, 96
Memory, 11
Metaphysics, 11-12
Metaphysics of society, Chapter 2 passim, 42
Might is Right, 108
Militancy, 34, 75, Chapter 7, 129, 132-33, 135
Militant order of society, 78
Mill, J. S., 98n, 128
Mind, 2, 19, 42, 52, 53-54. See also Consciousness; Epiphenomenalism; Spirit; Thought
Mind-body relation, 20-21
Monarchy, 90, 91, 131-32
Moore, A. W., 94
Moral chaos, 5
Moral cosmos, 3
Moral economy, Chapter 8, 124, 126-27
Moral freedom, 32, 44n, 69, 112-18 passim, Chapter 9 passim
Moral idealism, 6, Chapter 6 passim, 87, 93, 108, 110, 129
Moral ideals, 38, 74
Morality, 2, 5, 33, 37, 38, 41-42, 66-67, 82, 97, 105, 125. See also Ethical naturalism; Ethics; Impulse; Moral naturalism; Moral rationality; Political naturalism; Politics
Moral judgment, 41, 66-68 passim, 102
Moral naturalism, Chapter 1 passim, 25, 66-67, 92-93, 103, 116
Moral perception, 41
Moral rationality, Chapter 6 passim
Moral realities, 41-42, 128
Moral relativism, 102-4, 106, 130
Moral representation, 43, 86-87, 96, 115, 128
Moral science, 5
Moral society, 45n, 46, 53, 114-18, 121, Chapter 9 passim
Moral transcendence, 67, 108
Moslems, the, 95, 98
Motivation, 115, 117
Munitz, M. K., 23-24, 60-61, 116

Mysticism, 6, 60–61, 67, 72
Myth, 41–42, 82

National character, 50–53
Nationalism, 92
Nationality, 49–51, 55, 69, 133
Natural history, 11, 41
Naturalism, Chapter 1 *passim,* 9–10, 17, 23, 29, 56, 59, 64, 93. *See also* Ethical naturalism; Moral naturalism; Political naturalism
Natural right, 107–8
Natural society, Chapter 4, 47, 79
Nature, 2, 11, 12–13, 17–20 *passim,* 22, 27–28, 30n, 32–33, 35, 39, 42, 59, 64, 88, 107
Necessity, 13, 27, 28, 33
Need, 70, 104–5, 106
Negroes, the, 118, 121, 122
Neutrality, 69
Nietzsche, F., 107
Nominalism, 27, 30n
Normal madness, 94, 95

Objects, 18, 19, 27, 39, 65
Old Testament, the, 97
Ontology, 3, 59, 61
Order, 12, 27, 32, 70, 90, 95, 109, Chapter 9 *passim*
Orders of society, 78, 84
Oriental civilization, 7n
Other minds, 23

Parliamentary government, 131
Patriotism, 36–37, 47, 82
Peace, 70–73, 75, 76n, 77n, 124, 129, 132, 133
People, a, 117, 118, 120n
Perception, 18
Perfection, 37, 109. *See also* Ideal realization
Pessimism, 60, 135
Philosopher-ruler, 123
Philosophy, 10, 11, 28, 41, 134. *See also* Ethics; Philosophy of civilization; Political philosophy; Social philosophy; Theory of knowledge
Philosophy of civilization, 3, 7n, 9
Physical world, 22–23

Physics, 10, 11, 27
Piety, 26, 60, 122
Plato, 1, 3, 5, 35, 37, 39, 62, 63, 97, 121, 125
Play, 111
Pluralism, 4, 56, 59, 132
"Political" (*term*), 36
Political behavior, 12, 14, 80–81
Political ideals, 1, 64–65, 68, 73, 85, 97, 114, Chapter 9 *passim*
Political naturalism, Chapter 1 *passim,* 88, 92–93, 97, 99n, 103
Political parties, 36–37, 94–95, 131
Political philosophy, 9, 29
Political science, 1, 4
Political society, 34–37, 40, 41, 56, 97, 129
Politicians, 87
Politics, 4, 5, 9, 63, 84, 101, 106, 123, 128, 133, 134
Pope, the, 92
Post-rational morality, 6, 60, 91
Power(s), 3, 4, 13, 26, 28, 38, 40, 84, 103
Primal Will, 72, 83, 102, 111, 118, 132, 133. *See also* Will
Progress, 33, 56, 68, 72, 81, 103, 134
Proletariat, 69, 116
Propaganda, 85
Psyche, 21, 52, 80, 83, 104, 108, 123, 126
Psychology, 10

Race, Chapter 5, 73, 75, 85, 115, 117
Rational authority, 90–91, 96, 102, 104, 118, 124, 127, 134
Rational government, 63, 75, 96–97, 105, 106, 109, 117, 118, Chapter 9
Rationality, 6, 26–27, 33, 43, Chapter 6 *passim,* 84, 87, 91, 95, 96, 101–3, 112, Chapter 9 *passim*
Rational order of society, 59, 64–65, 75, 78, 108–9, 112, 115, Chapter 9
Reactionaries, 85
Reality, 18, 22–23, 27, 59
Realm of matter, 2, 26
Realm of truth, 10
Realms of being, 60
Realpolitik, 93, 103
Reason, 2, 13, 14–15, 18, 68, 73–75, 76n, 122, 128
Reform, 3, 34, 73, 81, 85, 90, 122

Religion, 1, 27, 47, 61, 66, 82, 91, 95, 97, 111, 125, 133, 134
Representative government, 69
Revolution, 85, 95–96, 97, 125
Right, 105–8 *passim*
Romans, the, 49, 130
Romanticism, 36
Russell, B., 29

Sabine, G. H., 79, 88, 90, 99*n*, 123, 127–28
Schopenhauer, A., 79, 104
Science, 1, 10, 11, 19, 21–24 *passim,* 27, 28, 38, 41–42, 44*n*, 66, 67, 82, 90, 95, 101, 134. *See also* Dialectical science; Political science; Social science
Self, 40, 52–53, 108, 113
Self-determination, 112, 118, 124, 130–31
Self-government, 86, 130–31
Social change, 34, 83, 103, 125
Social contract, 33
Social Darwinism, 51, 92, 103, 122–23
Social institutions, 12, Chapter 4 *passim,* 47, 55, 56, 70, 80, 90, 117, 125–26, 128
Social philosophy, 1–2, 9–10, 12, 29, 41
Social science, 5, 10–11
Society, 12–13, Chapter 4 *passim,* 53, 55, 73, 79, 115–17. *See also* Free Society; Ideal society; Instinctive society; Natural society; Political society; Symbolic society; Universal society
Socrates, 5, 62, 123
Solipsism, 23, 40, 52, 65–66
Sophists, 94
Sparta, 92
Soviets, the, 69, 92, 130
Speculative and critical perspectives, Chapter 1 *passim,* 9–10
Spinoza, B., 103, 104, 107
Spirit, 2, 21, 62, 68, 74, 108, 126. *See also* Consciousness; Mind; Thought
Spiritual freedom, 46, 93, 108–14 *passim,* 126, 127
Spirituality, 6, 32, 60–62, 72, 74, 110–11
Spontaneity, 34, 79, 80, 81, 111
State, the, 35, 97
Stoicism, 6, 64, 91
Subjectivism, 18, 21
Substance, 26

Success, 103
Symbolic society, 46–47
Symbols, 38, 39–40, 46, 127, 133. *See also* Ideal society
Sympathy, 72

Theory, 11–12, 39
Theory of knowledge, 23, 29
Things-in-themselves, 19
Thought, 13, 52, 54, 94. *See also* Consciousness; Epiphenomenalism; Mind; Spirit
Toleration, 72–73, 89
Tradition, 3, 46, 49, 51–52, 56, 64, 73, 75, 80, 84, 87, 90, 115, 117, 124–34 *passim*
Truth, 21
Tyranny, 81, 88, 96–97, 103–4, 130

Ultimate aims, 63
Unanimity, 52–53, 71, 92, 117, 129, 131
Understanding 28–29, 114
United Nations, 130
United States, 51, 118, 121, 122, 129–30
Unity, 41, 117
Universal government, 69–70, 130
Universal society, 71–72
Universe, the, 3, 28
Utopian ideals, 87, 94, 95

Vacant freedom, 111, 113, 129
Value, 2, 3, 37, 41, 62, 68, 89, 91, 102, 104, 107. *See also* Good; Moral naturalism
Value judgments, 70, 89
Verification, 19
Vital liberty, 108–15 *passim,* 117, 124, 126, 127, 129
Vivas, E., 115
Voluntary action, 83–84

War, 32, 35, 37, 41, 55, 70–73, 76*n*, 81–82, 129
Will, 8*n*, 21, 79, 81, 83, 86–87, 91, 98*n*, 104, 107. *See also* Primal Will
Will of the People, 132
Will to live, 93
Will to power, 93, 95
Work, 111
Working class, 122
World government, 69, 118, 124, 128–29

Yolton, J., 67